THE SILENCE
OF THE SEA

THE SILENCE
OF THE SEA

and other Essays

by

HILAIRE BELLOC

Essay Index Reprint Series

 BOOKS FOR LIBRARIES PRESS
FREEPORT, NEW YORK

INTERNATIONAL STANDARD BOOK NUMBER:
0-8369-2038-4

LIBRARY OF CONGRESS CATALOG CARD NUMBER:
74-107682

PRINTED IN THE UNITED STATES OF AMERICA

To

FRANCES PHIPPS

"THE SILENCE OF THE SEA"

and other Essays

These Essays originally appeared in The Sunday Times, "Truth", The Universe, The Weekly Review, and The Tablet, to the Editors of which journals I owe my thanks for their appearance here between covers.

CONTENTS

X CONTENTS

The Silence of the Sea

WHAT I most love in the sea is its silence: a sentence
that may sound strange till it is closely considered.
For the loud noises that a man at sea remembers are
not of the sea itself—no, not even in a gale of wind—
but of battle between the wind and what it encounters: rigging or the ship's side, or canvas, or the play
of a loose rope; the pouring of water taken in over
the lee or the strain of timbers. The sea of itself is
more reserved in its expression and, if it be alone in
its vastness, lives in its own communion.

Because the sea lives (while the land lies inert)
we cannot think of it as dumb: nor is it. But it speaks
in a veiled fashion as do the oracles of the Gods,
whereby it is one, the most universal and the most
august of the oracles: and indeed the oracles of which
we read were mostly not far from the salt and the air
of the waves.

*　　*　　*

The shores are sounding things; but only because
they are limits and bonds, not part of the Strength
of the Ocean. We, being creatures of the land, mostly
know Ocean from his beaches or even louder steeps
and stones; the tall cliffs that stand up to the surge
and re-echo the fierce come and go of a swirl over
uncovering rocks, or (rare but best remembered) the
tremendous booming of the rollers through half-
drowned caverns swallowing the rising tide. But the

1

sea, absolute in its unchallenged majesty, disdains to shout and clamour; it proclaims its advance, strength, and volume not by battle cries. A comber in deep water far from land is awful in the might of its advance; it rears into the sky and fills it, overhanging the hollow like a doom; but it does not threaten audibly. The sweeping crest charges over as might a line of cavalry, but without thunder; it resolves into a seething which barely hisses over the slope it had threatened and it dies in long streaks of almost silent foam.

When a man lying to, or barely making way up into the weather, has had a score of such liftings, his craft beneath him dipping and rising again, what stands in his mind when he looks back in memory upon the passage is not a fury but a ride repeated unceasingly as rank on rank of the successive ridges pass and slide below; and in most waters the days on which even so much of speech from the water reaches him are few. The greater part of his time at sea lacks even so much of any sound. There is for most of his voyage little answer from the Great Companion and no conversation but the murmur of water moving by, or, when he is working forward, the chatter of the perpetual wave at the bows when the water falls to either side before the stem and the ship sails on.

Also the sailor feels that an even tenor is normal to the sea and wildness exceptional. We think of the sea and storm together because the emotions roused by a storm at sea are of the strongest, and especially through the twin elements of suffering and danger, which between them make up what is most salient in human life (and a pretty commentary on human life it is that danger and suffering should so stand out in it!). The sea in storm is the sea "all out". It is the sea with its personality at the fullest; it is Poseidon angry and shaking the world. But not even the angriest of men or gods has anger for his daily mood. The common hour is serene or dull or level enough, and, though it impresses less, such routine of life forms the bulk of it; and indeed much of life is sleep. So with the sea.

* * *

Now if even in storm the sea makes less of cry or hail than any other creature in activity, in all other moods it gives out no voice at all. We may imagine its breathing but we hear none; though the large heave of it is the heave of a living breast. The sea contemplates itself and is content with that endless self-neighbourhood. On which account, I suppose, it is that you will hardly find any man long bound to a seafaring life but has something profound about him, more than landsmen have. He is clasped all round about by an immeasurable companion from whose communion he can neither escape nor would do so, for the sea conditions him, and makes him, and is with him all his hours—even on land, if he have known the sea long enough for the sea to have formed him.

The sea but rarely produces literary expression in its sons, "its human inhabitants", the sailors. Here

and there a book will be written or a poem created
by a man who is himself steeped in the sea. But there
is no human activity which has produced less articu-
late expression than seafaring. Writing upon the sea
has been the work of landsmen, not of men who take
the sea for granted. This is, perhaps, because your
seafarer has the sea all about and within him, so that
it is like the air he breathes; or it is, perhaps, because
the sea makes characters and men, not books. The
exceptions are few, and even in that small number is
there not a pose and an attitude not quite natural?
And this I think, this absence of human expression
communicated by the sea, is again due to the silence
of that immense world.

All will discover, on examining their memories,
that Silence, like her brother Darkness, is enhanced
and framed by slight exceptions. Darkness to be felt
must be what John Milton called the abysmal gloom,
"darkness visible". So also Silence is framed and
underlined by the least sounds accompanying it; and
the sea is the more silent for the hidden murmur of
it, the half-heard hint of small foam whitening in
the night for a moment and the whisper of a chance
air that is lost as it comes.

Those modern machines which have—or should
have—destroyed the peace of the waters, have one
odd good about them, which is, that they can sometimes give men opportunity for retirement within
their own selves; for they emphasize by contrast the
silence of the sea. That is even so with the little
motors which fishing vessels have now. Not that I

would praise these, heaven knows, or even apologise for them, but they do have that one advantage. But much better as emphasis to the silence of the sea was the hiss along the sliding water of the under-wave, which spoke of the sea's anger during storms.

I put it in the past; I say "was" and "spoke", but, of course, it still does so. The places where the silence of the sea has been broken by man are nothing to the vast fields over which it still reigns and imposes itself.

In good time the sea will recover all its heritage of Silence: the works of Man will have ceased, and the rattle of his metal contrivances. Then the Silence of the Sea will return.

Permanence

In times of grave public anxiety, after the tempest and destruction of universal war, after the expectation of further destruction and tempest, it is of high value to consider permanence, or what may be called the "Permanency of Impermanence". It is not only a consolation but a strength; a strength through the contemplation of a great reality and a steadfast truth. For though you may not affirm of any one thing in the mortal world that it is permanent, yet you may affirm of Permanency itself that it is permanent. You may repeat to yourself with confidence that the principle of permanence underlies all vicissitude.

So when we say to ourselves "When shall we see again the immemorial hills, the deep woods, and the quiet rivers undisturbed? When shall we again know Europe?" we are not asking a question in vain. There is a restoration, and lost things return. The earth upon which these human changes pass with such consuming violence has in itself a rhythm which endures and thoroughly belittles the accidents of excess. The sowing and the harvest, the new green and then the fall of leaves, the rising of a generation, its passing and its renewal, and out beyond all these the solemn circling of the Heavens—these are a foundation for the mind. Not that even these are eternal, but that they are in tune with the Eternal and a promise thereof.

*   *   *

Herein I for my part discover the principal value of history. History has many high values. It has been called by wise men "the principal school of politics". It shows clearly enough in its largest lines the limits to which the most generous enthusiasms must be confined, the term beyond which the most just of reforms may not venture, and the minimum at least of evil which human society must learn to endure. It adds a third dimension to experience; for as we garner a knowledge of reality from our daily contact with men and through observation along the course of life, we are still, as it were, only contemplating the surface. But when we call to our aid the record of centuries, depth is added to this mere surface, stuff, solidity. It becomes another and a greater thing.

History also gives you the knowledge of character. It gives you (if you read it with wisdom) an increasing appreciation of accident in human affairs. It is certainly a breeder of humility which, in its most general aspect, is no more than a seeing of ourselves (and of things) as they are. But still the principal value of history is the certain lesson it teaches that the underlying substance, even of society, certainly of the living world as a whole, is a symbol of permanence. It is a commonplace, but one of profound significance, that our minds find repose in the watching of ancient ritual, and most of all in watching that most ancient of all rituals, the recurrent dealing of man with the earth which made him, to which he returns, and whence his posterity shall spring.

*   *   *

I remember once in Barbary seeing a pleasing sight. It was near sunset upon the last slopes of the mountains where they melt into the sea-plain, fruitful and with many trees, orchards and vineyards. A man was ceasing from his labour of ploughing in his field. He prostrated himself eastward for the evening prayer. In that plain so slightly below me were certain ruins (scarcely visible) of a city deserted this thousand years and more. There had passed over that landscape every kind of revolution. Its Pagan gods had been forgotten long, long ago. Its Christian shrines and the high culture about them, the movement of the millions in its noisy towns, the march and trumpet calls of armies, the sails of galleys approaching harbour (a harbour long since ruined and unused), all these had gone their way. They had passed along their road, and had left not even shades remaining. But the man who had ploughed his field still ploughed it as did his fathers, and, in due course, he would gather his harvest. Soon the sun would set and the sudden darkness of lands under Atlas would fall, the last light would linger upon the distant summits, and then in a little while leave them also to look up towards silence and the stars. But the night would pass, and with the morning there would be new prayer in gratitude for the sun's rising and life advancing from the east, and the ploughing of the field would begin anew.

*   *   *

Even that recurrent ritual of man and the earth

will go its way at last, after we know not what aeons
of time. Yet there is about the aspect of such things,
the fields and their fruits, the procession of the hours
and the seasons, of the days and the works of the
days, something which makes them not so much an
example of mortality as a mirror of permanence; and
I would have any man whom our times have over-
wrought seek his nourishment again among those
peasants who have thus, since first men dwelt together
under laws and worshipped the divine, formed one
with the land they till. To such a scene would I come
back when the return of peace itself permits the
journey. I know where to find the place again. I
know I shall find it the same, or if not I, those who
come after me. It is in visions such as this that there
arises the high verse of mankind, the chief expression
of the soul, and itself, again, the most permanent, as
the things of humanity go. Even high verse is not for
ever, but its savour of perennial life, its timelessness,
is consonant with the all-enduring.

Nor does verse only spring from such roots, but
wisdom also, though of a general kind and not particular or applied. The wisest men, in the bulk, are
the men who have tilled the earth and whose fathers
tilled it before them, and the least wise, without a
doubt, are those who miss the meaning of that
august sequence in human affairs. Moreover, any
civilisation must be near its end when its cities out-
weigh its countrysides. It must be on the very edge
of dissolution when those cities have grown so huge

that they have lost contact with, and remembrance of, the furrows.

The Heavens, which are so much more ancient and will outlast that which they roof, are not themselves for ever, but they have "forever" written large upon them, for all men to read, and having read, to make seizin of their own dignity and of their immortal destinies. We, part of their household, may on that account repeat without fear that the immemorial hills, the deep woods, and the quiet rivers shall return.

Walter Scott

IN THE leisure of an ocean voyage I have re-read Walter Scott, and last of all *Kenilworth*. A number of days at sea is the best time nowadays for reading classical stuff, for life on land is so hurried that one can no longer savour there, as it should be savoured, the kind of English that delighted our fathers. It was written under conditions of dignity and leisure, and of dignity there is very little left on land, of leisure, none.

Walter Scott was, and is, a great artist. They say he is no longer read. I doubt that. I should like to see the statistics of sales before judging. But even if at the moment the younger generation have no time to read him, he will return. His talent is of the enduring sort because it flows upward from vision and power within. The machinery is old-fashioned, but the speech and action is alive. He sees the men and women whom he brings into action. They move and achieve their ends upon a stage which he has before his very eyes, and their motives are real. Also he abounds in the choice of words: that is, he is rich just where a writer should be rich, and such riches are the test of his vitality.

* * *

But I did not sit down to write of him as an example of high talent or genius—though he had that— but rather as a test and sample of the historical fiction on which the people of this country have been nourished for three lifetimes until it has become part of themselves. That is the chief interest of this group of our literature, for it is of profound effect on all the national life. For one person who reads history seriously with a desire to discover the past, as one discovers a country hitherto unknown, there are hundreds who get their idea of the past far more vividly, directly and permanently from historical fiction.

*   *   *

Now in historical fiction, in the writing of romances which purport to call the past to a resurrection, Walter Scott was a founder and nearly a pioneer. He had the rare distinction of influencing European letters outside his own country. He set a fashion and it took root, especially here in his own country and in England.

Historical fiction, of which men knew little or nothing before Scott's time, has become the most important literary form *politically*, from his time onwards, and still so remains. It makes people believe this and that about the stock from which they come and therefore about themselves. It convinces the reader of truth or falsehood about his own nature, and thereby forms the character of the society which reads it.

So true is this that history itself, to be conveyed to the modern reader, must come in the dress of a picturesque story. We no longer read chronicles, we read "Dramatised Biography". A book upon the past, however true, has value with us only if it is also lively, and however false has equal value if it gives vivid pictures of the thing imagined.

The consequence is that Englishmen, Frenchmen, Germans, the provinces of Christendom in general, have come to think of themselves not as they are and can see themselves to be, but as they think they were: as they have been told they were; and we in particular think of ourselves as Germans who came across the North Sea in little boats and, once established, went on being much what we are to-day. For it is the prime character of popular historical fiction that it "reads history backwards", thinking of the past as though it were the present.

That is why Sir Walter Scott is more and more true with history as he approaches the 19th century. His ideas on pre-Reformation Britain and Europe are absurd; his ideas of the transition when the Faith was being slowly crushed out of Englishmen by relentless government pressure, less so; his ideas of his immediate past exact and identical with reality.

In books like the *Talisman* and *Count Robert of Paris* he is moving in a wholly unreal world that never was or ever could be; but in books like *Kenilworth* he has a half-appreciation of what our forebears were like and what the England of their day would seem to one who should return to it in the flesh.

When I say that his idea of the medieval past was absurd, I do not mean his errors in extreme detail. These are often startling, but they don't really count.

He thinks that Byzantium had steeples and was Gothic, that the first Crusaders wore plate armour and were ablaze with heraldry, that French nobles of the 11th century had the habits of the 14th. But what really matters is not "examination howlers", but a misapprehension of the whole spirit of a society, and European society before the Reformation Walter Scott misses altogether. English society of the Reformation period itself he half understands.

* * *

Only half! If that. He thinks the England of 1575 divided into black and white: a mass of new Protestants (like himself) and a lingering remnant of quaint Catholics, picturesque, but out of place. Whereas the England of 1575 was, like all societies in revolution, made up of a large mass attached to their past in varying degrees and a small intense faction in possession of power and of gradually leavening the whole—but by force.

He thinks of the unhappy, diseased, bald, frustrated Elizabeth Tudor as of a majestic figure really governing England.

Thirty years after that date—the better part of an active lifetime—England was still full of the Catholic tradition, though it was fading. In the England of the Gunpowder Plot (which may well have been of the younger Cecil's own contrivance), the strongly anti-Catholic governing part was still only a minority, though a very large one. The body in some sympathy with the Faith was still half the country at least

though nothing like half desired a return, and the
bulk of men were already turning to the worship of
themselves and their national symbols.

* * *

Walter Scott—much more creative than modern
criticism allows—both started a movement and, unconsciously, marred it.
He launched that vogue for getting the past
through Romance, which has, since his time, become
universal. He was utterly sincere; all that he said he
believed, and if he had known more, his effect would
have less distorted men's view of their origin. For he
would have told whatever he knew and his readers
would have believed him. True, had he known all,
they could not have believed him because they would
not have read him. The real Catholic past of England
would seem too different from himself for a modern
Englishman to tolerate. But a large part of that truth
might have been established.

* * *

Is it now too late? That is a question no one can
answer—but this much is certain: the chances of
re-establishing true history are heavily against us.

The Under-dog

MANKIND HAS from the beginning of recorded history fulfilled an instinct for subordinating man to man. How many have found this laudable! Shakespeare had no doubt about it at all. "But for degree," says he, "where should we be?" "Take away degree," says he, "and all is a muddle and a mass!" Very true. But establish degree and the touching of one's hat to His Lordship (who made money so very rapidly and by such strange means) and mark what follows on *that*; legitimate anger (which is a good thing), envy (which is a bad thing), despair of advancement and (as William himself would have said—or perhaps did say for all I know), "captive good attending captain ill". Really it would seem as though there were here present what you always get in human affairs—and if so, that is not remarkable, for what you always get in human affairs is likely to crop up in any human affair. In all human affairs you get imperfection, pain, disappointment, and the rest of it; and there is always the impossibility of getting a good thing without attendant evils. Nor, by the way, is it true the other way about; for you can get an evil thing without any attendant good, except, indeed, this one attendant good, that suffering patiently borne brings (they say) a reward.

But as I was saying, there must be degree; there must be the top-dog and the under-dog, or (as it is put with golden philosophy in the "Wallet of Kai

Lung") "Lo-Chi's ceiling is Ti-Hung's floor". So far, so good. But the trouble is that once you have the top-dog and the under-dog, the fall of man leads the top-dog to oppress the under-dog. To prevent so grievous a result, much has been done; notably by saints, ordinary good men, and innumerable women of common sense. To prevent the oppression of the under-dog we have, to begin with, Charity, or rather, perhaps, to begin with, Humility—whereby the top-dog says, "The under-dog may perhaps be a better man than I, and more deserving." But on second thoughts I do not think Humility works exactly like that; I think it works rather more like this: "Mr Under-Dog looks very disgusting to *me*, but who knows how I look to *him*? After all, we are all Dogs together, and any day I may be the Under-Dog. The essential thing is that I am what I am, neither Top-Dog nor Under-Dog, but a miserable sinner full of fun."

The sensible women of whom I have just spoken (and who are, thank God, an enormous multitude) get over the difficulty by seeing all human beings as human beings; it would be no bad thing if men were to copy them in this habit so far as they can, which is not very far. For women, you will remark, though they have a violent appetite for titles and position and money, and the rest of it, have not that appetite for themselves, but for their children and their husbands, women being of their nature wives and mothers. They see human beings, and especially human beings of the opposite sex, as they are—and for my part I

wonder they survive it! Therefore you will find that
women, though they drive their inferiors hard, do not
think them essentially inferior; and that is, I suppose,
why women rarely rebel against women, though
manly men tend to rebel against men. The serving
woman complains and sulks, but rarely strikes.

Anyhow, the difficulty and injustice of under-
doggery is softened in all sorts of ways by the virtues
of charity and humility and by the presence of these
great herds of sensible women—for whom the Lord
be praised!

But still, the difficulty is there, there is the under-
dog and the top-dog, and the top-dog tends to oppress
the under-dog. The main cause of this defect in society
is oblivion. The top-dog forgets what the under-dog
has to suffer. Revolutions correct this evil, so do great
social strains of any kind, especially war; and among
various kinds of war, especially invasion.

It has been well said that all wars have an egali-
tarian effect, even expeditionary wars. When men
have suffered evil things together as men, and have
had to obey difficult orders from others not because
those others were rich, but because it is necessary to
have ranks in an army, they come to regard each
other as equals in essentials; and when the suffering
of war is made real to a whole society by invasion,
then indeed the mystical and life-giving principle of
equality takes on a force unknown elsewhere. If you
look about you, you will see that those nations which
have done the most fighting and have suffered invasion are the nations in which the doctrine of equality

and its practice is most alive—to the great contempt of the non-invaded, non-military nations, for whom the practice of equality is merely disgusting.

But let the great doctrine of equality flame forth as much as it likes, the top-dog and the under-dog remain; and with that division remains the tendency of the top-dog to oppress the under-dog, often deliberately, more often through negligence and routine.

Certain consequences follow, which I recommend to the dear reader lest in his dullness he should not have noticed them. One is that the very high moments of civilization are those in which the under-dog is getting a really bad time and the top-dog is thoroughly enjoying himself. It has been said, "No high culture without coolie labour"; or, in more dignified terms, "No civic virtue without slaves." Many other things have been said about subordination, and nearly all of them are half truths. But it is a full truth that if you look down history, all the periods of very great beauty or majesty in architecture, very great achievement in literature, have been periods of under-doggery run by top-doggery. To this I admit one exception and one only, the climax of the Middle Ages. Then, indeed, the mass of men in the Occident were worthy of the human name. But it did not last. Egypt, Syria, Rome, Greece and, for all I know, Mexico and Atlantis, were redolent of under-doggery.

The under-dog having been squeezed so as to get out of him the precious wine of civilisation, can at last bear it no longer. Then a change begins. Sometimes that change is violent—a Servile War. More

often it is only half-conscious and slow, but all the
more thorough. Servile wars are never won; poor
old Spartacus (I do not know how old he was; perhaps
he was quite young, I cannot trouble to look it up,
and in any case very likely nobody knows; I only call
him "poor" and "old" out of sympathy, the phrase
one uses to a dog—and he was an under-dog, though
a super one), poor old Spartacus, I say, came to the
accustomed end. When I was last in Castel Giovanni
(where I very much want to go again) I considered
Trinacria lying spread out below me, and mused on
Spartacus. I have not done so from the summit of
Vesuvius for two reasons; first that it is now a burning
place so that no man can go where Spartacus and his
fellows entrenched themselves; secondly because I
have never taken the trouble to climb the mountain
at all. He was defeated, though I cannot tell you
when without looking it up in a book of reference,
which I stoutly refuse to do—scholarship, I trust, is
on a greater scale than that! He was beaten; and the
Peasants' Revolt in England was beaten; and the
Norman serfs had their hands cut off, in spite of their
fine song of freedom—and so on, all along the line.
Servile wars never succeed.

But what does succeed is the fully conscious or
half-conscious strike of the under-dog. He gets tired
of under-doggery; he loses heart; the top dog takes
pity on him and applies to him a philosophy of
general-doggery wherein top-dogs and under-dogs are
all dogs together. Thereupon less and less work is
done, repose begins, and what I have heard called in

the universities, "The decline of material civilisation." Nay, I will not swear that I have not used the phrase myself when in a mood otiose.

Down it goes, does material civilisation, sliding along the slope which leads to the Dark Ages and to things done roughly, and to what the Chinese call "Can Do".

Now this is just what has begun to happen to us in Western Europe. Nothing is more interesting than to live history over again (as the man said who touched off a live shell on one of the old battlefields), and we are living over again today the middle of the third century. It does not follow that we shall see the fourth and the fifth. It does not follow that we shall see the Arch of Constantine replacing the Arch of Titus; but it looks uncommonly as though we should. Already people have got tired of rhyme; they have got tired of drawing things as they really are; they have got tired of painting with care, and of pretty well everything else that marks the civilised man. It will probably get worse (or better, whichever way you like to look at it); we shall probably go lower and lower, for the truth is that the under-dog takes his revenge—or shall we not say the Creator of both dogs takes it for him? "You have oppressed the under-dog" (says the Creator) "and now you shall gather the fruits of your oppression."

On Skulls

FOR SOME time past the world has been losing its interest in skulls—I mean of course *crania* (if that is the right plural for *cranium*, as I hope), not oars. In skulls, as oars, a large part of the world, in England at least, will always take some interest, especially in the Diamond Skulls. . . . At this point I discover that my old friend, the Demon of Inaccuracy, has fallen upon me again. The skulls with which a man rows are not, it seems, spelt with a "k". They are spelt with a "c". I had my doubts. I have just looked it up in one of my Books of Infallibility, and there was no mistake about it. I meant it for the best.

Be that as it may, skulls with a "c" still hold their place.

But the other kind of skull is not as much in vogue as it was. It went out almost altogether for more than a lifetime, until its modern revival—of which more in a moment.

The original and permanent popularity of skulls was as an emblem of death. They are with us, emblazoned in the arms of pirates, and sundry savages collect them. What made them really popular with us here in Europe was their use in religion, and especially in the iconography of religion—the Christian religion. The skull was the prime *memento mori*. No pious hermit was without his skull and many a great saint prayed with his skull to help him at his devotions. Yes, in the days when men kept

their eyes fixed on reality instead of bemusing themselves with imaginaries and make-beliefs, and what
some modern funnies call "wish-fulfilment", the
skull was popular indeed. He (or it) was a regular
ornament for graves, and I remember one famous picture in which a skull is brought in as a trick—a
strange object looking like nothing on earth turns
out to be a skull when you see it from a particular
angle at the side of the picture. The skull had other
uses. The pleasing Langobards drank out of it, and
pipe-carvers, after the introduction of tobacco, made
it a motive for their meerschaums. But its leading
use was still to symbolize and portray mortality, the
dread of which is the greatest of all follies.

Now when our forefathers went off the rails some
few generations ago, they preferred not to consider
the reality of mortality (although that phrase gave
them a nice rhyming tag all ready to hand to go with
it); they preferred to think of themselves as immortal; to play at immortality, if I may so express
myself; to shade their eyes from mortality; to hope
that perhaps, after all, it was not true, and to feel
most strongly that anyhow it was bad form to talk
about it. In that new school which was also the twi-
light of religion, the skull lost its place of eminence
and for a time was almost abandoned.

But your skull is a persistent fellow and he was
determined to get back somehow. He was watching
his chance! Since this main avenue was blocked to
him, he would try a side door, and very cleverly did
the skull find that side door. He got men to believe

that he was all important in *this* life, since they had ceased bothering about another.

The first step the skull took in getting his foot into the door which he found ajar, was called Phrenology. It was typical of the new time for it was a long word, and it was humbug. The idea was that by patting the peculiarities of a man's skull (or a woman's either, if she would allow the familiarity) you could discover the character of the skull-bearer. It was called in the vernacular "feeling your bumps", and from quackery it came as near as a toucher to being declared a learned profession. We were within an ace of having a College of Phrenologists and the letters C.P. after one's name, and a whole new department of medical science mapped out. There were diagrams printed showing what each of the bumps meant. I only remember one of them, which, like Phrenology itself, was most characteristic of progress and enlightenment and all the rest of it, because the name was immensely long and formed awkwardly and badly from a barbaric hotch-potch of Greek and Latin, the dead languages.

It was the bump of Philoprogenitiveness, and this extraordinary word was said to mean "fondness for one's children": a common trait, but not so common as it ought to be. This bump, I clearly remember, lay at the very back of the head. It was your bull-necked fellow, it would seem, who made the doting father, and the other sort—the man with the kind of pick-axe head like a stork, a common type—cared (we were told) nothing for his brood. I am not quite sure that this bump was not the ruin of the whole scheme, for it was a common experience that being fond of one's children had nothing to do with the shape of one's skull; and when that keystone had fallen the whole arch crumbled.

But Science is not to be denied. Science, the root of all our happiness, came in again in spite of fallen Phrenology. She pushed the side door wide open, did that majestic goddess. She came bearing a skull in her hand and a banner with a strange device: "Craniology", and as craniology skull worship had returned to bless mankind. It is now formally established. You can meet and revere a craniologist of eminence in every university of the world worth calling a university, and museums are crammed with skulls. For the skull (says Science) tells you what you are and why you are, what you can't help doing and why you can't help doing it, and in general has proclaimed itself the oracle of human life.

This glorious new science acquired what is proper to every true science—a whole army of technical words drawn from the Greek (to the honour of craniology they are not usually of that more common bastard type, Greek and Latin and vernacular all muddled up together), at least those which I can remember are true to form so that if you can't understand them but know the Greek alphabet you can find out what they mean in a Lexicon. Thus there is your *cephalic index* (here I must apologize, for the two dead languages here *do* appear side by side), and your *cephalic index* engenders your *brachycephalics*, and

your *dolichocephalics*, round skulls and long skulls;
and if you will take my advice you will strain every
nerve to be *dolichocephalic*, for it has been proved
in demonstration that the *dolichocephalics* are the
lords of the earth, while the *brachycephalics* are poor
degenerate creatures—in a word, foreigners. It was
only the other day that a learned man wrote to the
papers pointing out that the English were *dolichocephalic* to the extreme: which settles the matter.
He then went on to say that people with this sort of
skull could and did conquer all other sorts of men
and were as brave as they were adventurous, orderly,
kind, beautiful, humorous, clean, tall and good—and
he was one of them! Everyone got up and cheered,
and on that happy note I leave you.

Assault by Post

THE PHRASE "assault by post" was coined by a Regius Professor of English who knew what he was talking about, for he was himself the target of many such assaults and had a peculiar distaste for them.

Assault by Post is not necessarily the reception of displeasing letters. The letters may be very flattering and yet an intolerable interference with privacy and leisure. Among other forms of Assault by Post which men of this scholar's trade suffer is the request for advice on MS., for bibliographical lists, for opinions on the great (and little) writers of the past—and so on, down to mere demands for autographs.

But that word "autographs" opens up a wide prospect of mystery. We all know how the appetite for autographs began. Some very few famous men had left less than half a dozen specimens of their signature; even those who had signed their names thousands of times had signed them to documents which are not commonly seen or not preserved. Therefore rarity attached to autographs and at the same time no little honour. I remember the thrill with which I read as a young man a letter written by Thackeray to a senior relative of mine. There was a sort of incarnation about the business, as though what had been abstract or remote, a name, or a spirit, had taken on flesh before my eyes. Some years later, when I first saw a few verses of Tennyson which had been given by the poet to a friend, they gave me an appreciable

emotion: moreover, they were good verses. A little
later this feeling for autographs began to fade. A
little later still they bored me, and yet a little later I
began to detest them. There is something unreal
about this worship of relics attaching to characters
worthy perhaps of note but not worthy of worship.
Still, it is not difficult to understand the continued
respect for the autographs of men famous, if not great.
What *is* baffling is to understand the motive for col-
lecting the other autographs. The appetite is very
violent, however, whatever its origin. I have seen
over and over again men who could certainly not be
called celebrities, besieged by huge mobs as they came
out of lecture halls and nearly torn to pieces. It has
been touching to remark that the sick who could not
come would beg for the favour through a friend. It
made me think of the early Church.

With all this some of the best autographs imaginable have been neglected and a few deliberately
destroyed. Among these last there was an autographed
verse of Victor Hugo on the whitewashed wall of a
certain humble inn. Victor Hugo had written the
verse in anger; it blamed the inn fiercely for bad
cooking and dirt. The thing was written in pencil
on the white surface and the innkeeper was so proud
of it that he covered it over with some transparent
stuff, within a frame, and showed it to everybody who
visited him. One day a man who had heard about it
and travelled painfully to the place to look at it
found it had disappeared. There was a new coat of
whitewash, all shining and clean, but of that very

vain and very great poet not a line! The traveller was
astonished and alarmed. He found that some new
licensee had bought the inn. He asked his host what
had happened to the Hugo verse, and he was told
simply but firmly that it had been destroyed; not
merely whitewashed over, but chipped off and
pounded to dust before the new whitewashing was
undertaken. The motive of the murder was not concealed. The new innkeeper, a true citizen of a highly
civilized State, was a Parnassian. He detested the
Romantic school.

At least so he said—but I should not wonder if the
real reason were not simply Assault by Post. For indeed that inn must have been deluged with cards and
letters imploring him for details, for dates, for photo-
graphs. No doubt to the first owner who was proud
of his possession the assault was tolerable because
it was connected, however tediously, with glory, but
to the second owner it would not be tolerable at all.

Assault by Post, like so many evil things, blossoms
on a good tree, and is a fruit born of something as
worthy as it is itself detestable. For there would be
no Assault by Post were it not for two things combined, the great facilities of postal communication
today and the accepted social habit of answering letters. If it cost 2s.6d. to send a letter there would not
be much Assault by Post. If no one answered letters
there would be much less Assault by Post, even with
the post at 1d. in depreciated currency (that is, at not
more than .89872 . . . of a real penny at the time

of writing, and reckoning, as in duty bound, to five places of decimals).

The first cause, cheapness of communication, is, I am afraid, come to stay. The excellence of the English Post Office (that is a bit of collective boasting which I shall always support) is a wonder of the world. There is nothing like it in any other country that I at least have visited, and I therefore may humbly say that there is nothing like it anywhere. But the accompanying cause, the habit of answering letters, is on the decline, and just as evil has come out of good in the one case, so here good will come out of evil. For there is this good attaching to the detestable ill-breeding of those who are casual about their correspondence, that their example as it spreads helps to kill Assault by Post. To neglect answering letters is as unpardonable as to neglect answering a question by word of mouth. It is almost as bad as wearing your top hat inside the church at a funeral. It is a thing that used to be unknown, till it spread in the 'nineties. It was of course turned into a permanent plague by the universal use of the telephone. It has every conceivable disadvantage except one—it hamstrings Assault by Post.

There is an excuse today for not answering the importunate and the insulting correspondent if he be, as most such correspondents are, unknown to one. It is the old excuse "Nobody does that kind of thing now." Since nobody answers letters you need not have a bad conscience at leaving the assaulter in the air—even if he is of the inflamed kind who register their letters.

Unfortunately there is in the worst sort of these gentry a highly-developed cunning for compelling a reply. They will word the thing so that it is of importance to establish record of reception and even of comment. "I have told Lady Birdwhistlethorpe that I am writing to you on this matter and unless I receive your answer by the 23rd I shall advise her to prosecute." That form of aggravated Assault by Post is fortunately rare, but it exists.

Less virulent but tedious and a heavy burden to writing men is the magazine bundle marked outside with a little red hand stamped on the wrapper and the mention of a comment on the recipient's work. "See notice of your *Howl from Hades*." The vanity of us writers, however fatigued by age, is never quite extinguished. We say to ourselves, "My *Howl from Hades*, though it is far the finest piece of verse written in our time, has been boycotted: the boycott has broken at last!" So instead of throwing the bundle away you read through it, even though it be one of those gigantic trans-Atlantic compilements which are gradually de-afforesting the New World. The chances are you do not find the allusion to your classic poem at all. After wasting Heaven knows how much time in going twice and thrice over the huge mass of printed matter, you find at last, in small type under "Also received," and drowned in about fifty other titles, no comment, no criticism, nothing but the name of the masterpiece; a title put in an immense list, and nothing more.

Yes, Assault by Post is a very bad thing indeed. Like all bad things it will die in time, as good things do. Meanwhile it has, like most bad things today, one exception to its evil. Assault by Post gives the private citizen his chance of tickling up public men. You would be surprised to know, as I know by experience, the enormous importance a Member of Parliament attaches to a dozen letters coming in by the same post and protesting against him on the same matter. Though they be manifestly written by indurated cretins, some of them almost illiterate, they pierce to the marrow. So never refrain from writing to your local member. Give it him, as the Anglo-Saxons put it, good and hard. It is what he is there for. It only needs a few hundred people so acting out of ten millions to change the policy of this country—for the worse, of course, but no matter.

On the Use of Controversy

OF CONTROVERSY it may be said, as of all other things under the sun, that men are divided into two kinds —those who like it and those who don't. But there is this difference about it, that people either like it enormously or detest it like poison.

Now why is this? I think it is because controversy involves real conflict.

All men have in them an instinct for conflict: at least, all healthy men. Indeed, as everybody knows, "Conflict is the mother of all things," and as we are part of all things, we may be excused for liking our mother. But though there is this instinct for conflict in all men it is, in modern men, and particularly in us today, watered down until it often ceases to be conflict at all. You see that especially in the matter of games. Games are *sham* conflict. They are so sham that boys are particularly trained to avoid anger in games, and often grow up incapable of anger in real fighting. A game is necessarily restricted to quite artificial rules: one gains a victory in a game, but it is not real victory, it is only the scoring of points according to those rules. Wherever there is real conflict there is real victory on one side and real defeat on the other, attempted at the least, and nearly always real victory achieved or defeat suffered.

So it is with controversy. The end of controversy is the establishment of truth, and he wins who has used such arguments and evidence that no reasonable man can deny his conclusions. He is victorious who convinces the impartial auditor in the long run.

Of course the victor in controversy for the moment is not necessarily the final victor. The Achilli case is an example in point. Newman could not convince the court because the court was not open to conviction, but there is no doubt what posterity came to think about the matter. I think one may indulge the same consolation about many a modern issue in which what ought to have been the victorious side has failed for the moment. When time has softened the enthusiasms at work, reason does usually get a look in. You see that in the case of the Diamond Necklace, for instance, and it is true of a good many other historical debates which were passionate in their day. They have been settled once and for all, and we owe that boon to controversy. For it is a boon to have truth apparent and established.

There is also this good about controversy, that it has what few other forms of conflict have, and that is a highly comic side. For one thing, men are always amusing when they lose their tempers—anyhow, they are amusing in the eyes of those who suffer no consequences from their ill-humour. Now it is in the nature of controversy to make men lose their tempers, by which quality it breeds quantities of fun. The thing has been expressed in the phrase (I don't know who first used it) *Ille Sceleratissimus Brunkius*. Whoever Brunkius may have been (perhaps he was a German called Brunck; I don't know), his opponent evidently got very excited and came to regard him as a sort of criminal for differing from him.

Theological controversy is a fine breeding-ground for this kind of thing, and especially theological controversy based upon history. When the controversy merely turns upon an idea (as, for instance, whether the soul of man be immortal), though men will get very heated they can't appeal to obvious and material proof, so the man who won't be convinced remains unconvinced. There is, properly speaking, no victory in a conflict of that kind; I mean, no strictly logical or experimental victory on the lines of deductive reasoning, or of experience. The other man can always declare himself unconvinced. But appeals to some theological point upon which historical evidence comes into court is quite another matter! There, people do indeed lose their tempers gloriously, and I fancy the reason is this: that the victorious side having appealed to fact—not principle or faith—is felt by his opponent to be hitting below the belt.

I have often noticed how when something in dispute has been settled by the quotation of an indisputable text, the anger of the defeated is exceptional. It is as though a man felt, "I don't mind your making the gesture of hitting me and beating the air, but I do mind your beating *me*."

A man says, for instance, that a particular doctrine was not yet received at a particular date because there is no manuscript evidence thereof. His opponent trots out manuscript evidence which the other hadn't heard of, because it was discovered recently, and at once the fat is in the fire. Clinching evidence angers men so much that they will sometimes end by denying the obvious, rather than admit it.

There was a controversy some years ago between a specialist in biology and a superficial amateur on a biological point which was only indirectly theological, but sufficiently theological to rouse passion. The amateur said that a certain high authority had denied the descent of birds from reptiles. The specialist imprudently affirmed that the high authority had never said anything of the kind, for this specialist took it for granted that the wretched amateur could not know what he was talking about. Within that specialist's mind the descent of birds from reptiles was as firm a dogma as the descent of Englishmen from Germans was to the Oxford of my youth. Then the amateur quoted the disputed passage, verbatim. It was simple, direct and emphatic. The high authority had emphatically denied the descent of birds from reptiles. In vain did the unfortunate amateur plead his own ignorance and say, "I don't pretend to understand the evidence, I only know that this was what the high authority wrote." His opponent would not be comforted. He complained that the argument had been held in reserve and exploded under his feet like a land mine, without warning. This was indeed the case, but the complaint did not undo the force of the evidence.

As for the modern contention that controversy leads nowhere, that no one is ever convinced by it and so forth, surely it belongs to the general modern denial of the human reason. As the phrase goes, "It has long been proved there is no such thing as proof." As a fact—a mere fact of history—nearly everything we hold to be truth, save what comes immediately from the evidence of our senses, has been established by controversy. One need not go as far as to say, as did a friend of mine some few years ago, "I make men angry, and that is always a good thing"; but one can say that controversy, violent in proportion to the importance of its matter, has decided truth perpetually in the past and will continue to decide it for the future.

Therefore let all good controversialists take heart. Their effort is not wasted, even when they fail; for even when they fail they have served as the anvil on which truth was forged (I use the word "forged" in no ambiguous sense), and if they have succeeded, why then they have been the hammer.

So may all those be who are upon my side in any controversy. And very willingly will I accord to the other side the highest anvil honours.

William Tyndale

AT THE moment in which I write, the air is full of William Tyndale, one of the principal men of the early English Reformation.

He has, like most men engaged in that tremendous quarrel, become a myth, worshipped on the Protestant side both for the qualities which he had, and for the qualities which he had not. He ought to be equally famous on the Catholic side; but after the defeat of Catholicism in England and its rooting out (with very great difficulty and only after a hundred and fifty years of effort) by ceaseless government pressure and persecution, English Catholics grew unfamiliar with the details of the Reformation in this country. They remembered it as a victorious hostile event; they detested it of course; but they lumped it all together and did not concern themselves much with its details.

* * *

Now this is a pity, because people ought always to know their own national history, and (even in a battle they have lost) to distinguish between the various opponents with whom they were engaged. Of these opponents I myself find Tyndale one of the most interesting: the most interesting of all after Cranmer. The attitude he took up and his reasons for taking up that attitude and the effect he had were all of them typical of the time, and, like Cranmer, he is specially remarkable in this, that his effect was a literary effect. He illustrates "the power of the word"; the sentences he framed, and especially the rhythms, that is the swing of his style, have had more results, I think, than any other one thing in the whole business.

For Tyndale may properly be said to have created the English Bible, just as Cranmer may certainly be said to have created the Anglican liturgy. It so happens that by a strange accident the translation into English of the old sacred book of the Jews and of all the books of the New Testament—all that the Catholic Church calls "The Canon of Scripture" —gradually became, from rather less than three hundred years ago, not only the national book of the English, but, for most English people, their only book, and not only the book from which they drew their most familiar phrases but the book from which, interpreted in their own fashion, they drew most of their morals—including the conception that they were in some way a peculiar people, superior to the rest of the world, and under the special protection of God.

*   *   *

Now a book would not have that effect save through its literary power. The ideas in a book, or the statements in a book, if they are not put with literary power, could never persuade men as this book began to persuade a considerable group of English-

men from about 1620 onwards, quite half of them
a lifetime later, until it grew to be the familiar inspiration of most Englishmen soon after the year 1700.

Let it first be appreciated that William Tyndale
had not, any more than Cranmer had, or any other
of the reformers (save perhaps the Frenchman Cal-
vin), the idea of setting up a new religion. They
were occupied in what is called "reaction". They
found a great deal to condemn violently in the official
Church of their day; they rebelled against its authority because the agents of that authority were many
of them corrupt, and not a few false. In their anger
and revolt they attacked doctrine—though, strictly,
doctrine had nothing to do with their quarrel; but
they were not inspired by an enthusiasm for any
one new doctrine.

On the contrary, they differed among themselves
in every possible fashion as to what doctrines should
be followed. The one thing they had in common was
reaction against the established traditional body of
Catholic religion, with its courts of justice and its
hierarchy, its immense wealth and the rest of it. They
had no idea where they were going, and they certainly had no desire to break up Christendom, but
they were enthusiastic for a change because the thing
in which they had been brought up, and which they
still found so powerful all around them—the Church
—left them dissatisfied and angry.

Now all this is specially true of Tyndale, because
he was not one of those who initiated any new

doctrine. It is true that his motive in the work he undertook was a motive of rebellion. He wanted, as did all his contemporaries, to provoke men into violent protest against what he believed to be the decay and deadening of religion, and he was especially keen on producing this mood of revolt by an appeal to Holy Writ as against the living authority of the Church, which he thought had grown diseased and false.

* * *

Here one might delay to point out the astonishing irony that Holy Writ should have been used as a weapon against the Church. The old holy books of the Jews would never have been heard of in Europe but for the Church. It was the Church which had given them their authority, had said they were inspired by God and had added to them the New Testament. But for the triumph of the Church in the Roman Empire, Europe would for the most part have been completely ignorant of the Bible. Perhaps save for a few scholars, who would have been contemptuous of its various books, would have looked into them from curiosity, they would have thought the books of what we call the Old Testament to be the mere folk lore of a small set of oriental tribes, and what we call the New Testament nothing more than the fragmentary records of a small sect which had long disappeared. But the Church having triumphed, established the Bible and given it its authority, the reformers seized upon it as a weapon with which to attack the Church itself.

*   *   *

While the revolt against the official Church was brewing, in the two lifetimes before Tyndale's own, one main form of the attack upon traditional religion was to appeal to the text of scripture. For this purpose the religious revolutionaries would gather groups of men around them and read to them from Holy Writ passages which could be interpreted against this or that generally received doctrine. They would challenge the Church to show any mention of the Mass, for instance, as it was known in its full development, or of the sacraments (except adult baptism), or of Bishops and the priesthood, or, of course, of the Papacy. This was what was meant by "reading the scriptures to the people." The officers of the Church, that is the hierarchy, replied by restricting such readings and carefully watching the most dangerous form of them, which was the use of unauthorised translations.

*   *   *

We must remember that in the general story of the Bible all Catholic Europe had been steeped for fifteen hundred years. The Gospels and the lessons they teach were known then far more vividly than they have been known since, and the Old Testament narratives, proverbs, songs of praise and the rest were part and parcel of European life. They were not only alluded to as matters of course every day, carved up upon all sides upon public monuments. But at the end of the Middle Ages something abhorrent to Catholic Christendom was threatened: to wit, a break-up of society. Nothing would aid that break-up more than irresponsible translation of Holy Writ and asking every man to interpret it for himself, forming, as it were, as many Churches as there were people.

* * *

The movement of the reformers with its tendency to appeal to the Bible against the Church came to England late, as all European movements which arise on the Continent come rather late to this country. Tyndale himself was a young man at Cambridge just after Erasmus had worked at his Greek Testament there. He had not gone up to London till 1523, half a dozen years after Luther had begun the Reformation proper. He was beginning to associate with the more eager of the young men who looked for some change towards vitalising religion, but there was as yet nothing heretical about him. Indeed, as a priest he did what was normal to a priest of the day, that is, took a good lump of money—I think it was about £250 in our currency—to pray for the souls of a wealthy benefactor's parents.

* * *

A little later (in 1524) he went to Germany and to Wittemberg itself. He must have fallen under the influence of Luther's followers at that time, but there was nothing distinguished about him until, shortly after, he began to undertake the translation of the New Testament on his own account, into English. Then it was that he discovered that talent in which he was unique. He already probably had a little Hebrew, but for the New Testament that did not matter. He translated only the Latin and the Greek text as he knew them.

His motive in undertaking this translation was to promote the new opinions which he had embraced. For instance, instead of saying "church" for the Latin "ecclesia" he said "congregation", the idea being that a mere congregation would not have authority. Instead of saying "priest" for "presbuteros" he said first "senior" and later "elder"—and so on.

But the point about his translation was not its heretical quality, though that was the motive at work; the point was its magnificent style. It so impressed itself on those who came after that, nearly a century later, when the Anglican divines were issuing the Authorised Version, Tyndale's form of sentence, the music of his phrase, inspired the whole affair. It is the best example we know, I think, in literature (with the possible exception of Cicero) of the way in which one man's genius could impress itself upon a language.

*   *   *

There was already an English translation of the

Bible which was orthodox enough, and of course there had been for centuries translations of important parts of the Bible into the vernacular tongue, but this work of genius on the part of Tyndale (for it was a work of genius) had quite another appeal. No one dreamed in those times of printing without ecclesiastical or State authority, any more than we think to-day of coining money without State authority. Therefore, Tyndale's unauthorised translation of the New Testament had to be smuggled into England, it was tracked down and destroyed when it could be caught; it was even bought up by ecclesiastical authority in order to be destroyed (thus providing Tyndale with money). St. Thomas More engaged in controversy upon it, and no one can read the arguments used on the two sides without seeing that St. Thomas More had much the best of it.

* * *

By this time Tyndale was marked everywhere, but especially in England, as a prominent religious revolutionary. But though he lived abroad in order to escape persecution, Henry VIII favoured him because, although as a rule the king detested the new heretics, this particular heretic had written a book affirming the absolute right of the king to govern his subjects in all things; in other words without submission to the Papacy. It is true that he said in the same book that the only authority in religion was the Bible, and the Bible as interpreted by each individual

man, but Henry forgave him that on account of his
king-worship.

*   *   *

A change came when Tyndale, two years later, in
1530, opposed Henry's divorce. That was the one
point on which Henry VIII always got excited. He
knew that the affair with Anne Boleyn had made
him ridiculous and unpopular, and anyone who
rubbed in that ridicule and unpopularity drove him
half mad. He tried to get Tyndale extradited by the
sovereign of the Low countries where he had taken
refuge, but that sovereign was the powerful emperor,
the uncle of the lawful queen whom Henry was
trying to get rid of, and he was not likely to hand
over the victim.

Henry's next idea was to get him kidnapped and
brought over to England, where he might have dealt
with him at leisure. Perhaps he would have done
what he did to Katherine of Aragon's confessor and
slowly roasted him alive; for when Henry's vanity
was at stake there was no limit to his extravagance
in cruelty. But Henry never got hold of Tyndale.

*   *   *

What happened to him was this. He took sanctuary
in what was known as the "English House" at
Antwerp. It was a house left as a kind of hostel for
harbouring Englishmen abroad, and the emperor
felt he had no right to invade that sanctuary. He was
lured out of it by a certain Phillips, who may or may

not have been acting for Henry, but who at any rate had a grudge against Tyndale, to whom he owed money, and Phillips betrayed him by a pretence of zeal for Tyndale's new heretical opinions. (By this time Tyndale had gone to the extreme left of the reformers and was denying the Real Presence.) Once he was out of the house the emperor's police pounced upon him in the spring of 1535, when he was a man of about 40 or over. He was imprisoned, strangled and his body burnt on October 6, 1536.

* * *

That, I suppose, is why the *Dictionary of National Biography*, which is cram full of such errors, gives August 6 as the date of his death.

Bunyan

THERE IS, at the moment in which I write, a certain mild interest arisen in a possible discovery of John Bunyan's will; probably by the time this appears in print the discovery will have been settled one way or the other. So far, it seems that scholars doubt the authenticity of the fragment—but the news gives me an excuse for musing upon that capital figure in English letters.

I had the good fortune to receive the "Pilgrim's Progress" at an impressionable age. I was, if I remember rightly, about nine years old when my nurse read it to me from end to end, and it left very vivid pictures in my mind. Indeed, I think it is the chief quality in Bunyan, that he can thus exercise that most powerful of English talents, the visual imagination. In this edition of the "Pilgrim's Progress" there were prints of an old-fashioned kind: I knew nothing, of course, of their date, but I remember them well. Apollyon vastly interested me and Giant Pope was the most impressive figure of the lot. Christian, himself, I could make nothing of, for that draughtsman of long ago had rendered him too mild for my taste; his eyes were cast up to Heaven, and that is an expression, which I make bold to say, no young person likes. For the young know nothing of tragedy, let alone despair. They suffer acutely, but they do not realise the suffering of others.

I say again, any man is fortunate who has had in

childhood any one of the classics put before him; later on he will not have time, or if he have the time he will no longer have the malleability to receive the stamp of them as it should be received. In later life we get occasional rare and disconnected revelations of really good writing; we retain them, they furnish our minds, but they have not the edge and sharp outline of the earlier things. Moreover, it is one of the misfortunes of our time that it has become haphazard in its selection of first-rate things. This is not to say that we moderns never recognise a contemporary masterpiece, still less that only second-rate or third-rate things appeal to the public to-day; that sort of judgment is common enough, but false. What *is* true is that in the mass and rapidity of modern book-making the critical faculty is swamped. I could make a list in my own case of, perhaps, a dozen quite first-rate books which I have come upon by accident since my maturity and not one of which has taken a popular place; but it is also true that I have come across a greater number of first-rate books in my maturity which have been recognised, and, as a rule, recognised at once.

What it is that makes a book "take" can never be fully known; the factors are too numerous, too elusive, and most of them too dependent upon fashion— a thing no one can judge save those who have experienced it. But the quality which makes reputation can be judged in part, for some of the factors are clear enough.

There must, in the first place, be lucidity. Much

turgid stuff has acquired a passing fame for the wrong reasons among a few, and the many will often repeat the judgment of those few, although they themselves do not really share it. But a great popular success such as that of the "Pilgrim's Progress" is never to be had save by something written in a fashion which the common reader can at once and easily understand. Of course, lucidity is a mere negative quality; it is a necessity for enduring letters, but the mass of un-enduring printed matter has it as well; most railway tickets are lucid and most posters. But though it is common to the best and the worst lucidity is neces-sary to the best if it is to live.

*   *   *

Another quality more valuable and more rare which must be present in any book that is to capture a very wide general public is consonance with the spiritual atmosphere of its moment or, at any rate, of the moment in which the reading of it begins to spread. This attribute is not necessarily praiseworthy; more often it is the opposite. Of all the winds of opinion, let alone of enthusiasm, very few blow steadily. Now Bunyan, in his "Pilgrim's Progress", wrote with full sincerity and intensely in communion with a very widespread mood of his time. It is bad history to call that mood universal in the England of Bunyan's formative years, let alone when, at fifty, he published this book. On the contrary, the quasi-Calvinist attitude towards religion (which in this country we call "Puritan"), although it held the mind of very large numbers, did not hold the mind of the majority—for what that may be worth. The point is that it was held with a sort of fierce appetite; it had what we call to-day driving power; moreover, it was most widely spread just in those classes which best guarantee permanency. It was widely spread among the smaller landowners, among the skilled artisans, the commercial classes of the towns, and—what is important—the teachers. Further, there was no counter influence of anything like the same voltage.

The very many to whom this mood was distasteful expressed their distaste in satire or mere contempt, sometimes in active aversion, but they did not set up against the Puritan code, which was vital and active, or even against the Puritan doctrine, another rule of life and another set of definitions.

*   *   *

But when all is said, the "Pilgrim's Progress" digs itself in by style, that much maligned excellence: the choice of words and their order. Therefore it is that special passages (what were called half a lifetime ago "purple patches") are the necessary floats or corks by which a network of writing is supported on the waters of time. All must have noted that the number of such passages in any classical writer are few, and the mere fact that the same excerpts are perpetually reappearing in the praise of great prose or verse, is proof of this; as is also the working of our own minds. For whenever we have laid down a book of prose or verse read through, we cannot, in the nature of things, remember it as a whole, save in a general and half-conscious fashion. But we do retain vivid possession of certain passages standing out.

Now, in these, Bunyan was singularly fortunate. I say "fortunate" because the thing is indeed a matter of good fortune: of luck rather than of choice. The ancients were right to speak of inspiration. They were even right when they personified the muse.

John Hawkins

JOHN HAWKINS returned to England from the third of his slave raids, in January, 1569.

*　　*　　*

Meanwhile a thing of great importance had happened in Europe. Certain Spanish ships bearing treasure for the payment of the Spanish troops in the Netherlands had run for shelter into Plymouth and Southampton towards the end of 1568. They ran for shelter because the Channel was infested by Protestant rebel pirates from France.

The Spanish Ambassador asked Elizabeth's leave to land the treasure and convey it by road to the Straits of Dover where it could be safely escorted over the narrow seas to the Spanish Netherlands on the other side of only 30 miles of water. Elizabeth, of course, was glad to give leave to a friendly power making so reasonable a request, but William Cecil, not Elizabeth, was the person who really governed England. He had long desired to free himself from the sense of obligation towards the King of Spain, especially as relations between the two countries were getting strained since the seizure and persecution of the Catholic legitimate Queen of England, Mary Stuart, by William Cecil himself was now well afoot.

*　　*　　*

Cecil therefore invented an excuse for detaining the Spanish bullion ships (which had on board about

£1,500,000 of our money) and, treating Elizabeth's orders with contempt, he said the money would be held until he could find out to whom it really belonged. Elizabeth, of course, had to give way as she always did, because she was in the hands of this man and his set.

The anger of Spain at this mixture of hypocrisy and theft may be imagined, especially as Cecil was showing himself more and more the determined enemy of the Catholic religion and would root it out of England. The anger of Spain was made the more intense because lack of the money to pay the troops who were in the Netherlands necessitated a tax on the inhabitants of those provinces, which tax provoked a rebellion.

*　　*　　*

While things were in this state, John Hawkins saw an opportunity of killing two birds with one stone: he would recover the ill-gotten gains confiscated by the Spanish pirates, he would at the same time offer his services to the King of Spain, bring ships and men whereby, with the aid of the Spanish support, he could restore the traditional Catholic religion of the English people, to which the great mass of that people was still attached.

This is the critical point in the whole story, and we must be very careful in reading it to understand what historical evidence is.

*　　*　　*

Historical evidence consists in documents interpreted by our knowledge of the nature of things. It
must consist in documents, because there are no wit-
nesses remaining alive to give us personal evidence,
but the mere evidence of a document is not sufficient
to establish a point. If a man writes a letter on a
particular date telling one that he met a man 200
years old, and giving no corroborative evidence, we
disbelieve the document because what it states is
against all our experience.

In the same way we must allow in ordinary human
actions for the ordinary human emotions and not
accept extravagant explanations which would only
be true if those emotions were not present. If we
find a man murdered and the valuables which were
on his person in the possession of a man running
away from the scene of the murder, we conclude that
the man running away was, if not the murderer, an
accomplice. We want special proof to believe it was
a coincidence and that the man running away was
innocent.

* * *

Now the known facts in the case of John Hawkins
are these. *He did certainly approach the Spanish
Ambassador and suggest the bringing of English ships
and crews to the King of Spain for the purpose of
supporting the widespread Catholic dissatisfaction in
England and of restoring the old religion.*

We also know as a certain historical fact that the
Government of Spain in the long run accepted the

offer. We also know that John Hawkins had been, before that, in correspondence with the King of Spain: that each party knew all about the other. We further know that John Hawkins was, as might be imagined from the character of his activities, profoundly indifferent to religious doctrine one way or the other, and intensely occupied in making as much money as he could as quickly as he could and in the easiest way he could.

So far, so good.

The next thing we know is that John Hawkins, months later, was hauled up before the Council under an accusation of treason. The next step is that William Cecil, the master of English policy, is found after this using Hawkins for the purpose of obtaining correspondence from the Government of Spain which he, Cecil, could then examine at his leisure in order to discover what that Government was up to.

*   *   *

Here we have to decide between two possibilities. One probable, the other improbable. The improbable possibility (and it is highly improbable) is that John Hawkins, out of religious enthusiasm or what not, lent himself *from the beginning* to some wonderful secret plan of Cecil's for duping the King of Spain.

The other possibility—and it is so highly probable that it is virtually certain—is that John Hawkins had approached the King of Spain on his own, that his correspondence had been tapped by Cecil's ubiquitous spy system, and that then the life of John Hawkins had been forfeit. Cecil could do what he liked with him, and used him to carry on a renewed correspondence with the King of Spain, and so make the Spanish Government a dupe. In other words, that John Hawkins, having been found out in a piece of treason to Cecil's Government and his life being at their mercy, had to consent to do their business, and having begun the correspondence in order to make as much money as quickly as he could by serving the King of Spain, was compelled, after he had been discovered, to do whatever Cecil told him and to act as a Government servant and spy.

* * *

The whole issue lies between these two conclusions: Did John Hawkins approach the Government of Spain "on his own", was he caught doing this and thenceforward used as a servant and a spy by Cecil? Or was he from the beginning a man devoted to Cecil's Government and the Protestant religion and willing to run the risk of his life for the purpose of serving both?

The question has only to be put in order to be answered.

In the absence of documents proving the exceedingly unlikely alternative we must conclude that John Hawkins was doing what he could to make money quickly out of the King of Spain, that he was caught in the act, and used after that as a cowed Government spy.

*   *   *

If we are to accept the other hypothesis we must believe that a man who had never bothered about religion suddenly became enthusiastic about it; that a man who had kept up (as we now know) a secret correspondence long before this affair with the Spanish authorities, was innocent of any attempt to deal with them; that he was indifferent to large sums of money payable for his services; that he cared nothing for the hatred felt towards Cecil's tyrannical Government by the mass of the English people and their attachment to the ancient religion, still so very strong: remember it was less than 10 years since the forcible suppression of the Mass.

We must further suppose that the seizure of John Hawkins and the bringing of him before the Council was all a piece of play-acting, and we must imagine a whole previous intrigue between Cecil and Hawkins for which there is not a shred of evidence.

The conclusion to which any impartial reader of the evidence is necessarily drawn is that Hawkins had everything ready to bring the ships and the crews to the King of Spain, was caught in the act, and then used as a decoy by Cecil in order to discover the policy of the King of Spain.

*   *   *

That is the common sense view to take.

But in history one must be rigidly just. It is not an absolute certitude. There *may* exist somewhere documents hitherto unrevealed which prove the official story as it is told, for instance, in *The Dictionary of National Biography* and in pretty well all our official textbooks. There *may* be letters somewhere, or reports of conversations or notes—some kind of evidence—that Cecil used John Hawkins from the beginning, but no such evidence has ever been discovered.

The right way of treating the incident, therefore, as historians, is to say that we cannot be absolutely certain which of the two theories is true, but everything points to the probability of Hawkins' having tried to strike a bargain with the King of Spain and then having been caught *and*, after that, used as a counter-spy by William Cecil and his gang.

One should add that the "alternative hypothesis", though exceedingly unlikely, is possible, that sufficient evidence might conceivably be found to support it, but that none has appeared in nearly four centuries.

*   *   *

Now the point of the whole incident is this—Not whether the much more probable hypothesis be true, but the way in which our official history deals with this affair.

All our official historians talk as though they knew for a matter of fact that there was evidence for the improbable hypothesis against the probable one.

They all pretend that from the beginning of the affair John Hawkins was the devoted Protestant servant of William Cecil and his policy. And they go on saying this, although they have not a shred of evidence in their favour, while all the real evidence is the other way.

One may sum the whole thing up thus: John Hawkins is asserted in our official textbooks, from *The Dictionary of National Biography* downwards, to have been the willing ally of Cecil when all the evidence goes to show that he was rather the unwilling servant compelled to obey Cecil by terror *after* his effort to bring ships and men to the King of Spain in aid of English Catholicism had failed.

But why do they say this? Why do they fly in the face of the existing evidence and put forward as historical a state of affairs for which they not only have no proof, but which is the opposite of what all the existing proofs point to?

The answer is simple. They want to suppress evidence for the strong Catholic feeling in England at the time. They want to make out that the English people in the early years of Elizabeth supported William Cecil—which is a falsehood. They want to make out that even from the first years of Elizabeth, there was a grand saga of seafaring heroism proceeding on the Protestant side. They want to identify this with the spirit and destiny of the English people. They want to hide the part played by Philip of Spain in supporting Elizabeth and to antedate the quarrel between Cecil and the Spanish Government. In other words, they want to present a myth as though it were real history and this, in plain English, is telling a lie.

*   *   *

That particular lie is only one example of very many in the false story of the Elizabethan times upon which two generations of Englishmen have been brought up, but I think it is as good a particular example as you can get.

The Unfortunate Great

GEORGE VILLIERS (on whom I have just read an admirable monograph) might, by one little twist of circumstance, have remained with his fellow-countrymen among the greatest of Englishmen. He certainly deserved such a place. He has left but a doubtful ambiguous record praised by very few, and lacking any principal monument.

To begin with, his time might have been almost designed for the misconception of his true self and of his talents. It was both a magnificent time—his boyhood was the middle age of Shakespeare, his most active years were the prelude to the Civil War, he was a slightly younger contemporary of Cromwell—and a time of creative change in everything English: in English religion, in the structure of English society, in the launching of the English future. It was the beginning of the English Colonial expansion and the dawn of that decisive business, English power at sea. His own life and fate turned upon a foreign maritime expedition wherein he showed genius.

He might have stood at the head of the long absorbing story which tells of English expansion overseas. As it is, he is but a half-remembered figure. He certainly wears no laurels, still less any of that deceitful halo which tradition has set about the head of many lesser men. And the reason he has not had his due is a triple accident: the accident of unmerited defeat, the accident of historical writing (of an official legend), and the accident of an early death.

He was one of those men also to whom chance had given vast early opportunity. The two things often go together: an exceptional start, a destiny unfulfilled. In those days when Kings were everything he had risen like a meteor through the favour of a King. Oddly enough that favour was merited, for he could organise, he could understand, and he could command. When those three things are true of anyone he may achieve anything. He understood beauty, and with his immense new wealth he collected in those very first years of manhood works of art that were the wonder of Europe. He was courageous, he was clear headed. In his brief career under arms he proved himself a great soldier. Had he lived he would have proved himself a great statesman. He was assassinated just before before all this might have matured, and just after an effort at victory had for the moment failed, but might so easily have been renewed. He was still in the thirties when death took him at that one stroke of Felton's. He was the very man to have stood at the side of Charles I in the great struggle that was preparing. He was but eight years older than that unfortunate man, and intimate and trusted he might have doubled and surpassed the aid which Strafford, his exact contemporary within a year, afforded to the Kingship of England. He resembled Strafford also in the strong swarthy physical type of energy for which he stood—and all that was thrown away.

What a sight it would have been to have seen him, in the strength of his fiftieth year, at the opening of the Long Parliament! Later, if he had failed to redress the fortunes of the Crown, what a duel between him and Cromwell, who would have hated but respected an opposing energy comparable to his own! He lived not even to know that there was such a man as Oliver.

He was unfortunate also in his pictorial record. More than one great man has been enhanced by remembered representation of him permanently before the public eye. Not so with Buckingham. To see the fullness of him in portraiture you must go abroad, and you may know him best perhaps by the Rubens drawing at Vienna. No popular image perpetuates him among his own countrymen. And yet he was of the sort that his countrymen will always praise in action. He had just that lineage, just those bodily aptitudes which they will respect and follow, just those failings which they are inclined to pardon.

One might consider a group of such men: Marceau among the soldiers, among the poets Keats. They are few, but they shine. And of them all the writer has the better fate, especially the poet. For what *he* does is not subject to decay nor even to what is more fatal than mortality, misunderstanding.

In his way, I am not sure that Henry V of England, the Plantagenet, does not come into that category. He had the double advantage of victory and of very great verse to perpetuate him. But he also died long before any real achievement. He died at much the same age as did Buckingham, in the mid-thirties. I can conceive him as having held that double throne over all the West which had been the ambition of his ancestors for 300 years. But all he left behind him was a puny, insufficient child and a disloyal wanton widow, to whose vagaries with an upper servant we owe the Tudors. Should we beckon Gustavus Adolphus to join the group? He, too, was doing mighty things when he was struck down. Shall we reckon Charles the old or the almost forgotten De-saix? All those three men suffered an identical fate: killed suddenly in battle, their corpses stripped upon the field by robbers, and lying for hours naked in their wounds—and it was Desaix who won Marengo, not Napoleon.

It is unwise, in considering frustration of any kind or failure, to make it only part of one blind process which destroys men and their works haphazard at any age at any point in their development: for there is destiny. It is wiser to look upon the few examples of those who might have been what they were not, and who came so near to completion and fulfilment, as special tragic figures, as exceptions which show off the general fortune of the famous. It is wiser also to consider achievement in any form—I mean public achievement—as negligible compared with that un-known particular hidden thing, the soul that has borne fruit. But the examples of disappointment and the empty grasp teach the lesson of reality and put man in his right order. Yet I can but consider that to any one of such unrewarded men some knowledge before death of later glory among their fellows would have been sufficient. Few, or perhaps none, of them had such an advantage, and men of high action who die contented are so rare that you will hardly find them.

On Diarists

I GIVE my readers fair warning that, sooner or later, I am going to write on Samuel Pepys. I shall not be the first to do so; but Mr Bryant's book sent me back to that admirable civil servant's self-communings, and what a writing-man gets by his reading cannot but come out in his writing: it is the unfortunate itch of my trade. Meanwhile, I would like to potter about a little at large on diarists.

I take it that there are two kinds of diarists: those who intend to be read by others and those who do not so intend. Now diaries intended to be read by others, even if they are kept from the public eye for a lifetime or more (as was the excellent and well-bred practice of our fathers), have about them an element of untruth. The moment a man talks to his fellows he begins to lie. This is a truth, and not such a hard truth as it sounds, for it would be impossible to address one's fellow men without some measure of slander and spice, and even of advocacy, and these three things—let alone fifty others in human conversation (amusement, astonishment, vanity, anger—even charity)—impede the narration of truth and distort that exact balance of values wherein truth consists.

But a man who keeps a diary for the best of all purposes and the most exact, the most consonant with the true nature of a diary, I mean a diary which is written with the object of nourishing the writer of it alone, of calling back his past to life, of confirming the unity of his own soul and of preserving such fragments of happiness as life affords—such a diarist determined that none other than he shall read what he has written, does indeed do the very best with his pen.

I live in hopes that diaries of this kind will continue to be discovered, as they have been discovered at intervals in the past. They invariably open a window upon history, even though that history be recent. They are superior in this respect to correspondence, however intimate, because correspondence involves another mind. Correspondence is invariably affected and warped by the spiritual presence of the addressee. And that is why the most vivid, the most vital, form of correspondence, love letters, are for the most part gibberish: so much so that if a young man write two love letters and put them into the wrong envelopes the recipients will as likely as not each take his own missive to be intended for him or herself.

*　　*　　*

That old diaries shall still be newly discovered as time goes on I am the more inclined to believe, because I came on one myself quite a short time ago. It had been printed for private circulation at the end of the eighteenth century, and apparently had never been bound or circulated in any numbers, for I could not find by advertisement or through acquaintances the trace of another copy. What that diary was I keep to myself, for, as it came from a private connection, it is not for the general eyes. It was kept by a woman, the lady of a large house, and deals with the things which were intimate to her alone—the bringing up of her children, the management of her servants, her garden, and (a great deal of it) her directions to the cook and her recipes for the kitchen.

But an ancient diary, even though it deal only with details of such a kind, is always crammed with information worth having. I can remember only one diary which was too dull to read, and that was not ancient but almost contemporary. It came out as memoirs, and there was very little in the memoirs that was not also in Baedeker. But a secret diary from the same pen would certainly have been worth reading. Diaries of the long past are fascinating, almost in proportion to the lapse of time between their day and our own. One thing they do which is invaluable, and that is to present *unconsciously* the change in social mode between their time and ours. The witness who does not mean to create this or that effect, the witness who presents his evidence unwittingly as it were, is the most valuable witness of all. I remember coming in a diary of the late seventeenth century (Evelyn's, if I remember aright) upon a passage in which the writer speaks of casually passing in his walks abroad a burning at the stake; an unfortunate woman convicted of poisoning her husband was being burnt alive. The man who has left a record of this little incident at Smithfield, which (again if I remember aright) he came upon as he sauntered to the house of Grinling Gibbons further on, records his emotions of distress and pity—which is to his credit. The striking thing for a modern reader is the limitation of such distress and pity. He is sorry for the victim, but not extravagantly sorry; he finds the sight of that burning miserable enough, but not, as we should find it in England to-day, intolerable. I think it fair to say that his emotions were very much those which a kind-hearted man would have to-day on seeing a gang of convicts being led out of a train into the Black Maria. He was shocked, but not bowled over.

*　　*　　*

Why are there so few diaries? Because mankind, and even womankind, lacks the industry required. Most people have enough routine in their lives and certainly enough leisure to keep up the daily entries; but they have not the tenacity sufficient to keep abreast of the work. For one thing, there is no money in it. And yet I suppose every man who has lived a long life, especially if it be of a half-public sort, regrets his lack of a diary. However wrong-headed his judgments may have been, however superficial his appreciations, he would have preserved out of ten thousand chance happenings a hundred or two which would have been of permanent value to him. The memory preserves these in a healthy man, but not long enough; the memory does not do what the written record does; it does not fully evoke a whole mass of detail and make it come to life out of the past. Moreover, memory is treacherous; contemporary record, if it be written for the private eye, alone is a trustworthy informer and preserver.

Imaginary diaries, books cast into the form of diaries, have, I confess, never satisfied me. The fault is, I suppose, in myself, for I know that they have satisfied many competent judges of fiction. But for me they are marred, either by being set in a remote past, the diction and furniture of which must always seem artificial and stilted, or (being set in a time nearer our own, as in the case of some modern novels so written) they deal with events either too diffuse to be worthy of record or too consecutive to create the illusion of a real diary.

Anyhow, whatever we have of diaries, the tragedy remains and returns in them, the note of bitterness that is in all human things, but also another note: "Would that I had kept a diary," says nearly every man at last. *Utinam.* It is a recurrent cry of humanity.

Boswell

IT HAS always seemed to me that in time of stress there are two kinds of reading to which a man may profitably turn for his recreation. The first is matter directly connected with the strain imposed upon him, the other is that sort of book which becomes immortal through a discursive character about it, so that you feel, while you read, as though you were engaged in conversation rather than upon literature. During an excursion of some length upon the French front, in the midst of travel some of which was arduous, I could put to the test *this* judgment: that either technical matter or a text quite remote from one's surroundings and powerful through individual human interest alone, were the alternatives required for the repose of the mind. As to the first, I read the history of sundry places which it was my business to visit. For the second, I read the Eternal Boswell. It is of the second that I write to-day—quite inadequately, but as a testimony to its power. For I could read Boswell in pretty well any circumstances, I think, save shipwreck.

* * *

I know not how it is with other national literatures, but certainly it is a mark of English writing that it throws up almost isolated, strongly individual, things which stand out not like a work of art or a perfection, but like a personality; so that we may

71

compare the landscape of English Letters, surveyed over the last three centuries, to one of those country-sides in which the heights form no continuous chain, but stand individually, each alone. This character in English Letters I have always thought to be a func-tion of that power in the English mind by which it concentrates on some restricted department of reality and, conversely, instinctively avoids types. There is a weak side to this, a drawback, because a judgment which avoids generalisation will with difficulty mas-ter a broad plan and see things in their main outline. But the strong side, the good quality, of this particu-larism is the vividness with which it apprehends its subject. It has been truly said that English fiction is a gallery of living men and women who never lived.

You cannot put the masterpieces in any rank or order, for each is a species of its own; but, for my part, if I were asked to single out the summits which have most impressed me, I should point to "The Diary of a Nobody" and to this same book on which I am now musing, my companion in so exceptional a journey, Boswell.

*   *   *

There is in Boswell full proof that sincerity is a necessary ingredient to good writing. It is not enough, certainly; most of the tedious stuff is intolerably sincere; but the core of this particular masterpiece is sincerity, and through sincerity it has not only lived, but grown. I venture to say that Boswell's book be-comes larger and larger among its peers with every

decade that passes. The curious will observe that in
the whole range of it there is not one piece of fine
writing, there are not three lines anywhere in which
one might so much as suspect concern with the
writer's art. Boswell is wholly occupied with that
simple, but fundamental human need—worship. He
is absorbed in his devotion. It fills his every interest;
it gives edge to all that he hears and sees in connection with his idol.

Let me assure such of my readers (and I hope
they are many) as have never themselves ventured on
the unpleasant task of literary composition, that it is
a refreshment and a delight to come across matter
wholly free from it. It has been said of Boswell that
he writes as a man would talk, perhaps one might say
as a man would talk to his secretary, saying, "Oh!
By the way! Here's another letter you might copy out
for me." But I think the truth is rather that Boswell
writes as a man thinks. There is no sequence save
that of acquaintance with his subject, the natural
process of time and the stream of acquaintance.

It goes without saying that such virtues are based
on the supreme virtue of simplicity. There are many
people to-day who have forgotten what the word
"humility" means. To such I recommend the reading
of Boswell, wherein they come across the completely
humble, because wholly devoted, mind. I had almost
written that Boswell possessed humility in the heroic
degree and therefore deserves to be canonised: the
more so for his little frailty on which we need not
pause. Whatever its degree, it did not prevent his

adding one considerable glory to the treasury of his country—for one may talk of a common country here without straining the point.

*   *   *

Boswell's humility, of course, is thrown into relief by the abominable manners of the older man. There is something almost repulsive about the way in which Johnson opens one letter after another with common abuse and does not seem to know he is doing it. The contrast between this rudeness and the recipient's gratitude is never painful. It all seems part of the game, and if one did not know how thoroughly artless was the Boswellian soul, one might almost think that the brutality of Boswell's god was an artifice, directly introduced in order to throw into greater relief the magical meekness of the disciple.

For, to the wise, Boswell is the hero of that famous book, not Johnson. Indeed, I have heard it disputed whether such a being as Boswell has drawn for us ever really was. I have heard the paradox maintained that Boswell's "life" is a masterpiece of creative fiction and, what is more, that, but for Boswell, Johnson's name would not be remembered. I cannot, of course, subscribe to that whimsy. The strength of the features and of the character behind them, the soul of Johnson, have been expressed for us in another medium than prose. Still, but for Boswell, what figure do you think Samuel Johnson would cut today?

There are collaborations in all the history of

writing. Some few have proved fruitful. There is the collaboration of two working in one authorship without distinction of the strands which each contributes to the whole. There is the collaboration of the learned man and even the expert with the ignorant, but creative, man. And there is always the collaboration of every writer with the society in which he lives: especially collaboration with the spirit of his own country. But the most subtle collaboration of all, the most creative, is the collaboration between the writer and his subject. That collaboration Boswell enjoyed abundantly. What landscape was to Milton, what urban eccentricity was to Dickens, what the mathematic was to Pascal, that the personality of Samuel Johnson was to James Boswell. It fed, it invigorated, it moulded, it provided full purpose. The chances are that no one else could have played Johnson's part, and very probably, almost certainly, no one else could have played Boswell's part in the arrangement. Whereon hangs an interesting side issue: "What are the chances, one in how many million, of such a juxtaposition?" I cannot answer that question, nor can anybody else; but we can at least say that the odds are so heavy that "chance" is the wrong word, and some more old-fashioned title such as Providence, the right one.

Jane Austen

READING Jane Austen the other day, I considered the interesting truth that certain figures of fiction are immortal and permanent companions.

There is nothing original in that remark (thank God); it is obvious and has been made a thousand times. I make it again now for the sake of carrying on with a tradition. But my particular point is that a certain, a particular type of character in fiction has a special sort of immortality: I mean that type of character in fiction which has been described with great care, minute detail, exact observation, no emphasis, no exaggeration and yet a certain terseness so that there are no unravelled edges left over, no new, weakening interest through the use of too many words. Miss Austen excels in this method, and it is this which has given her the place she so well deserves in English letters. She wrote only of the world she knew—the same is true of Trollope, who was vague and doubtful on very rich people and almost oblivious of people below the rank of a large farmer. The same is true of any one of forty first-rate spectators of mankind and recorders thereof, native and foreign. But Miss Austen has this special virtue that she is always on the level of her subjects. They pass before you in an orderly, exact, sufficiently restrained procession. Therefore they live.

They do not live with any violence of effect, there is no deep graving, there is no high relief; indeed, I have found the best metaphor in which to express this admirable achievement is to compare it to an inlay of silver upon pale wood. Yet though there is no attempt at vividness, no underlining, none the less her immortals remain immortal. I confess that I cannot always remember which character is which. In the same way, one cannot always remember the names of the people one met in a large number of guests at a country house, but Miss Austen's ladies and gentlemen (they are never anything else, though she delights in ticking off those who are "not quite") are people whom one would at once recognise after an absence if one came upon them again. Their voices are subdued, their gestures not more than indicated, their emotions refined—to use no worse term. But they are there all right, and we shall meet them, I trust, in the better places when time is fulfilled and all our companions gather round us for ever.

I wonder whether she knew she would triumph? Of course she did not know it fully; no man or woman engaged on the tedious and dreadful trade of writing knows what fruit his or her tree will bear. Most people who write, I think, exaggerate the value of what they have done. At any rate, no writer can possibly judge the permanence of his or her achievement. And whatever permanence it has is a very mortal permanence and a very circumscribed one.

In Europe to-day, divided and unstable, there is no general area over which even the best literary effect can spread. But anyhow, this woman is an *alpha plus*.

Of that there can be no doubt, and she has taken her place because she has excelled in the quality of proportion—which is another way of saying in telling the truth. But I have taken her only as a text, for up and down the various literatures of the past and the present—such few of them as I can read—I note a great crowd of imaginary men and women thus called to life, and to a life far less ephemeral than our own lives here on earth. They go on; they do not decay; they are fixed. It is a pretty irony that the soul of man whereby all human things are accomplished should be encased and bound up with that which perpetually changes and perpetually fails, that which takes so many years to achieve even an insufficient maturity, and which then falls off so certainly and so irrecoverably from its highest moment. Here again I am not saying anything new. It has been said before; it will be said again, but it is worth saying. It is a pretty irony, I say, that we, who can make all things (very nearly), cannot make ourselves; that we who carve stones which endure till the children of our children's children have forgotten who did the carving, and we who write verse which the fifteenth generation after us, knowing no more about our very selves than the stocks and stones around us, still quote with lively delineation; we who build the palaces and the towers, and we who vibrate with active life projected into symbols destined for endurance, we ourselves do not endure.

I have delayed so long upon the immortal light and shade of Miss Austen that I have now exceeded the limit I had intended, for I desired to talk of others who have done something of the same sort in their various ways. But of these there are very few who have produced the quiet images of living men and women. Most writers have produced either types of heroes or villains or figures which are not animate but used for the purpose of a plot, like puppets on the stage, and the very greatest writers (by whom I mean the poets of the epic sort and the dramatists to whom all mankind is beholden) also throw out for our attention brilliantly lit, strongly coloured, heavily shadowed characters. Yet, somehow, few of them are the men and women whom we know.

None will deny (I hope) the place of Dickens in the English language, or deny the place of Chaucer; many would deny the place of Racine in the French language, and some would even deny the place of Molière. The epic writers who have set before us statues rather than human beings do not concern us in this regard. They make no pretence to living flesh, even of the pale fictional kind. They work in marble. But among all those who have put words upon the lips of men and women, not actually in being, not physically present before us, but figments of their own minds, I know, in my limited reading, of no one that has achieved the same result as this woman.

It is on this account that I read her not only for the exquisite pleasure of her art (whereof I am convinced she was in the main unconscious), but also in order to learn wisdom from her and the understanding of my fellow beings: especially the understanding of women.

For it is the value and the glory of Miss Austen that she tells us poor beasts, the other half of mankind, not only what women are, but what women think about and what they care about. Young men do not think it is important, as a rule, to explore that spiritual country called womankind; but if they live long enough they will know that only by some dim comprehension of it can men of a certain age find their way about.

Miss Austen tells a man who reads her (and I fancy she is more read by men than by women, and I feel sure that in the future she will be still more read by men than by women), Miss Austen, I say, tells us about her own sex, and she does this in two ways: first, by betraying in her own comments what women think important about their brothers, their husbands and the other men about them; secondly, by what they think important (but usually in a bad way) about their own kind.

I think it true to say that a number of her women together may often be compared to a gaggle of cats. It will seem that these beings (to me they are mysterious, but to her they are an open book) are perpetually worrying about what we think of them! God rest their souls! It is true the other way about—we bother too much about them. But I noticed only this morning, turning over one of her pages, a charming and comforting reflection. She says of one of the men in her books that one of the women in her books who came across him paid no attention to what a certain gentleman thought on any matter, because she did not care enough about him—not in the sense of affection, but in the sense of attention. So speaks this ambassadress from her own sex to mine, and I will not be so ungenerous as to leave her without a corresponding reply.

My dear Jane Austen, we also do not care a dump what any woman thinks about our actions or our thoughts or our manners unless they have inspired us to—what shall I call it? It need not be affection, but at any rate attraction, or, at the least, attention. Once that link is established, we care enormously: indeed, I am afraid, too much.

This is a very great secret; it has never been told before, and perhaps I am breaking the rules of a trade union in mentioning it at all. Now that the cat is out of the bag, let it miaou. I do assure you, my dear Jane Austen (and I know with what care you are reading these lines, because there was never an author yet who did not read with care an appreciation of his or her own work), I do assure you, most admirable Jane, that only our interest in one of your sex breeds any attention of ours to what they say or think or do. When we are indifferent to a woman, her beauty matters not a hoot—nor even (alas!) her wisdom. It is something other that does the trick; what it is, their guardian angels only know. I don't!

Anno Domini

YOU WILL have occasion for some time to come to write, more than once, the figures 1939. Whenever you inscribe this mystic number breathe to yourself some word in memory of the man to whom you are indebted for that date. His name was Dionysius and he was an abbot in Rome during that strange time when the history of England disappears and runs underground like the river Mole: the darkness between Germanus and Augustine. For he flourished (as the phrase goes) about 1400 years ago in the earlier part of the sixth century, and it seems that the one date about him on which we can be certain is that he was dead by 544.

Now it was his computation of the date of the Nativity—or rather the Incarnation—which became gradually accepted throughout Christendom . . . very gradually. You cannot say that it had become common everywhere until well into the Crusades nearly 600 years after his death, and I have read somewhere that his fixing of the era by which we now everywhere reckon the years was not taken over fully in Spain until the fourteenth century. You will find what I suppose to be the decisive phrase in Migne, that half of Migne which prints the Latin Fathers, and in the sixty-seventh volume thereof Dionysius writes:—"We did not wish to mix up our memorials with impious and persecuting men" (he means, with the Roman emperors of the earlier pagan times), "but rather did we choose to note the sequence of years from the Incarnation of Our Lord Jesus Christ." And that date he put just after the middle of the eighth century from the traditional founding of Rome. A.U.C. 753-754.

* * *

He was almost certainly wrong as are most pioneers and founders. How wrong we do not know. There are all sorts of guesses based on all sorts of slight fragmentary evidence. For instance, we have the death of Herod in 4 B.C.; but those who understand these things (which I do not pretend to do) will have it that his "year one" may have been anything from four years too late, as is more probable, to seven years too early. But it took root and you will not shift it now, neither you nor millions with you: not all the Revolutionaries, nor all the over-learned. I suppose it is about as firm a thing as the past has left us, is the computation of the years A.D. and B.C.

This Dionysius was called, or nicknamed, "The Little," "The Short," "Exiguus," and it is as Dionysius Exiguus that he is remembered to distinguish him among the other Dionysiuses, from the Areopagite and the martyred apostle of Paris onwards. The little we know about him is mostly from a few phrases written by a fellow student of his, a younger friend who counted much more than he, Cassiodorus. Cassiodorus is the larger figure, partly because he was richer, partly because he did much in the politics of his time. In part also because what he has to say

about the motley Imperial garrison of barbarian soldiers then in Italy and their chief has helped a certain modern school to crack up the Germans at the
expense of the rest of us: a favourite game of the
nineteenth century. This friend, Cassiodorus, with
three generations of great wealth behind him, full of
music, writing much, wrote thus about Dionysius—

"There was also in my time among many great
men Dionysius the Monk, a Scythian by race, but
altogether Roman: most learned in Latin and Greek.
He lived his life god-fearing like a high master. There
was in him a great carriage but with it great simplicity, doctrine, and humility. I would like to say
more about him but I must get on with my work."
Whereupon Cassiodorus goes on to say more about
him, after having promised not to do so, which is
what one might expect of a public man dealing with
public affairs. The rest that he has to say about his
friend ends up very prettily—even finely: "He has
left this evil time of ours and has been received into
peace, and we must believe that his conversation is
now in the household of God."

*   *   *

But Cassiodorus could not guess how vast a fabric
would extend from the labours of this one man. He
did not know that all these centuries after the whole
world of our white civilisation would be taking his
date for our Era as a matter of course; nor did
Dionysius himself know it. Had he known it, it might
have spoilt his humility, though it is even said that
he called himself, or was called, "The Little" by way

of humble modesty. I prefer to believe that he was so called because he was not tall. Thus he falls into the company of those many fixed names (or great men if you prefer to call them so), who had the advantage of few inches and therefore much energy; strong hearts with less work to do than have the hearts of taller men. He may be greeted by Napoleon and Wellington and Charles I of England and Canute and any number of others who perhaps when they were boys were ashamed of their stature but found, later on, that the defect was an advantage.

I have said that his system grew slowly in public esteem. I read that it was first adopted at all widely in England under the influence of Bede, the Venerable Bede, about two centuries after that system had been lodged, or at any rate crystallised. From England it spread southward, and Gaul was taking it up in a beginning sort of way within a lifetime, but the Papal Chancery did not use it for another 200 years.

No one ever made it official and no one can properly tell you how it developed roots so firm and so penetrating. But I say it again, it is established now more decidedly than any other act of all our long story.

*   *   *

There is no more favourite diversion among pedants than the changing of things which it should rather be the duty of the learned to conserve. If everybody has been saying "Magna Charta" for generations it is a delight to them to call it "Carta". If our fathers said and wrote "Thomas à Becket" they must needs make it "Becket". Thus also they have monstrously stuck in an E after the A of Alfred just to show that they had read Anglo Saxon, and as for the "Senlac" of Vitalis instead of plain Hastings I have written on this so often that I dare not repeat the objection now. They have turned the pronunciation of Latin (whereof we might have made a common tongue for general intercourse) quite upside down, consonants and vowels and diphthongs, so that my contemporaries can remember at least three quite different ways of pronouncing the simplest Latin phrase, three different fashions succeeding each other in the short space of one human life. Perhaps a fourth is coming along. One can never feel safe in such things. They white-wash every villain. They degrade and malign every hero. They have shifted the Tin Islands from Britain to Spain, and one of them not so long ago solemnly propounded a theory that the works of Aeschylus were written by Euripides, telling us that the effort was not beyond "a precocious southern boy". They are capable of anything—save one thing. They will never shift A.D. and B.C. They will never turn this year of grace into 1943 or 1932. It has come to stay.

Such is the glory of Dionysius Exiguus, and since it is proper that glory should be made eternal by the Poets, let us remember him so. As Diodorus Siculus is immortalised in the lyric "Diodorus Siculus, made himself ridiculous", so let Dionysius have his deathless rhyme: "Dionysius Exiguus was wrong but not ambiguous." With that tribute I leave him.

On New Years and New Moons

THE NEW YEAR is over-valued. Properly speaking, it is not there at all. It is a whimsy; it is an imaginary; it is a fiction of the mind; it is a convention; it is a fraud. I wonder that the Jobbernols, that vast crowd who object to anything that is not tangible and cannot be tested by experience, have not protested against it before now.

The new moon is something real. She hangs in the sky a tender crescent, a sickle of ethereal silver magically transmuted under the evening into gold. She lacks only a hammer of the same metal to make her a symbol of all that is best and noblest in the New Everything. She is (quite rightly) openly worshipped by many savages and secretly by most civilised men as well, at least, of those who inhabit the countrysides and have not been sterilised by girders and cement (to which let me add the daily papers, a highly antiseptic influence). The new moon has been hymned, and most deservedly so, for she is really there; indeed, I myself have seen her more than once. The new moon is worthy of our adoration because she is real.

Of course there is illusion even about her, as there is illusion about all her sex; for I am assured by the learned that the new moon is only a slice of the old one, and that the old one is there all the time; but, anyhow, the light on that lovely little, exiguous little, gradually brightening little arc is real, if, indeed anything told us by our sense be real. We can hold on to the new moon firmly as something that we know (though we are not allowed to touch it), and the way in which the new moon, just at her virginal best, dies away into the western mist and disappears from our sight is admirably pathetic. It is a theme I should recommend to the poets had they not already got hold of it in herds and were they not still grinding it out by the page-full. It is true that I have seen none of her in what is called "Modern Verse"—but then, modern verse has nothing to do with poetry.

*   *   *

So much for the new moon which has led me astray from my theme, fascinating me as is the habit of Goddesses. (If you doubt this get someone to read you a text-book on mythology or to sing you the song in the "Belle Hélène," which, though of the Second Empire, and, therefore, Victorian and until lately mixed up with the general curse of horsehair furniture and plush upholstery in general, is homely and human and so not to be despised. The tune is lively, but it needs to be sung with feeling and go. It is forgotten now, and those who still remember it are too old to sing.)

It is my business to return to the New Year, though, to tell the truth, I see no reason why I should. A man writing on some strict subject, such as "The Morphology of the Cacchenidae in their relation to the Jurassic Formations," must stick to his subject or be torn to pieces by infuriated pedants. But I am under no such obligation to-day, still less are my

readers. If I like to wander at large, I may. Nor need
they be fatigued by constraint to a particular path,
though I fear it must be a little tiresome to be dragged
through a mass of undergrowth. But no matter. If we
do not begin to talk about the New Year we shall not
get to it at all. So here goes.

I say that the New Year is a whimsy; an imaginary;
a nothing. It is not there at all. You may receive it
with all manner of ceremonies; you may treat it with
solemn ritual; but all that is part of the myth-making
of man. It is indeed part of reality that The Seasons
do actually pass and return in a circle, a ring whence,
if you like, the word "annual". The days will actually
grow longer (thank heaven), and then they will get
shorter again after Goodwood. There is a rhythm
about all this which I do not pretend to understand
but which is part of reality; and we human beings,
bound in by reality and confined to it until we get
away to better things (for I mean by "reality" all the
business of this world), must set boundaries so as to
know how far we have got along the round of the
works and the days.

*   *   *

For the moment we have fixed on a certain day,
the first of January, which in its turn is not there.
There is no January. It is one more of those imagina-
tions, without which in our weakness we cannot live.
I would rather believe in a Janus with two faces (for
I have met such people) than in such an abstraction
as January.

Moreover, any day out of the three hundred and sixty-five and a quarter—to be accurate 365 days, 5 hours, 49 seconds and a "snift"—which is the present length of the year (but that is changing and may change again if something comes to trouble us from outer space), would do for a starting point. Not so long ago, March 25, called by the old-fashioned and by rent-collectors, Lady Day, was the first of the year. And from what I have read the Chinese have yet another day altogether. And the Mohammedans and the Hebrews are said to have a calculation of their own, to which they are welcome. You would certainly find if you searched throughout mankind that New Years were almost infinite. So let us be grateful that we have a solid and rooted one of our own, on which there can be no doubt. Let us also withstand all efforts at changing our ritual, for by ritual men live. It must have been a dreadful wrench when the English suddenly lost eleven days rather more than two hundred years ago. And what good did it do anyhow? Except, of course, to debtors who were paying interest. Or to their creditors? I cannot be troubled to calculate which.

*   *   *

A New Year has this useful thing about it, whether it be Mohammedan, Hebrew, Julian, Gregorian, Chinese, or Choctaw: it makes man remember and regret his follies and his sins. Never forget the great saying that when a man comes towards the end of the downward slope and sees before him the open gates of the marble tomb, he finds on either side of him two groups of companions. They talk to him continually and leave him no peace: on the right side his follies; on the left his sins. If we did not become familiar and conversant with these ultimate companions we should make very poor wayfaring with them at the end. And as, before the end, we lose all other friends and fellowships, let us at least be conversant with these and learn to know them each by name and to grasp them familiarly by the hand, turning to the right and saying, "Good-morning, my dear Folly Number 8! Let us talk over the matters that concern us . . . But, excuse me, my left sleeve is being pulled." "Good-morning, Sin Number 368. Remember me to all the little sins."

I say that at the New Year we enter into preparatory companionship with our follies and our sins. Wherefore idiots on this occasion make good resolutions. They had far better make money (which lasts) or hay while the sun shines. But the sun does not shine at the New Year, and there is no hay, except what is already stacked under its thatch in the rick outside the yard.

Fun for Clio

FOR a man who really likes history as I do, that is a man who likes finding out what really happened and even occasionally saying so (to the vast irritation of many) the times in which we live have one great compensating advantage for their beastliness. They are vulgar and they are chaotic, they are murderous, they are dirty, they are atheist, they are intolerably wearisome, they have every vice, but they are a magnificent aid to the understanding of history.

For instance, nothing used to puzzle an older generation more than wars of doctrine, or as they were called in the past, "religious wars". In what mood could men have been to suffer and inflict such awful things for the sake of an idea, an invisible thing, an imagination? Well—now we know. The whole of Europe is involved upon a war of doctrine, slowly spreading exactly as the old religious wars spread; dividing the citizens of every country into hostile camps exactly as did the old wars of religion—and though the present perils and horrors are not called wars of religion even fools are beginning to see that they are at least wars of doctrine.

On the one side men say that the family and the freedom of the human will and therefore property are things worth dying for; on the other side men are saying that all these interlinking things, because property is among them, must be destroyed. On the one side men not only will die themselves but will kill other people to make the family and economic freedom safe, to maintain property and contract and the right to bequeath wealth to one's children and to own one's hearth. On the other hand men say, these imaginaries, these superstitions, are mortal to the real good of men, and must therefore be destroyed. We will die and we will kill others rather than let such doctrines survive in activity.

And then there is this other example—credulity. How (said an older generation) could people ever be so credulous as to believe the fables and legends of the past; why was the great enlightenment of the Renaissance so slow in coming and its full development in the 18th century more tardy still? Well, today we have only to look about us—people can be got to believe anything whatsoever by mere repetition. Our great urban masses swallow the most fantastic legends and become furious if they hear the absurdity denied. Motives are solemnly affirmed which any child could discover to be false; and actual things are affirmed (as having happened) which neither happened nor conceivably could happen. For instance, during the war the vast mass of English people believed that Russian troops had passed through England on their way to France. They also believed that the census figures of the Reich had been faked in order to conceal the man-power available for the Prussian General Staff. A smaller but still respectable number of English people believed that two Angels had appeared at Mons. A poet has recorded the illusion.

> There once were two angels of Mons,
> Who appeared to the Dean of St. John's;
>   And to no less than three
>   Maiden ladies at tea,
> And a couple of celibate Dons.

This kind of thing is explicable, you may say, through the strain of War. But there is any amount of it today, quite unconnected with any strain at all. Men will delight to repeat that the Hippopotamus is descended from the Kingfisher, and when you ask for the missing link they will tell you that they haven't got it but they know very well it is to be found somewhere and will turn up any day. Or they will tell you that the Universe is expanding, and when you ask, "Into what?" they snarl! And why do they snarl? Because all men snarl when something they have bolted whole is disturbed—men do not like their digestions interfered with. They do not merely admit, they fantastically believe that two things cannot happen at the same time, or that there can be two different kinds of time in two different places. They talk of imaginary units of matter, which no man ever has seen or will see or in any way attested by his senses, as though they were golf balls. Visions of the past were nothing to these certitudes of the present.

Are there any other modern examples recalling those old records of human vice and folly which we call history? There are dozens. But one will do to wind up with. An older generation marvelled that men should unquestioningly obey a King who claimed absolute Divine authority for his mandates. Today you find men falling into exactly that state of mind in the presence of what they call a majority. All sorts of evidence is shouting at them to show them that this word "majority" has no meaning because it may be of any kind whatsoever—a majority of men or a majority of women or a majority of men and women combined, or a majority of those who care, or a majority of those who want to express an opinion, or a majority of those who are bored stiff with having to express an opinion, or a majority of those who don't express an opinion but simply make a mark on a bit of paper. They may mean a majority of a thousand and one to a thousand, or a majority of nine out of ten, a majority of citizens or a majority of professional politicians, a majority of murderers, a majority of savages, a majority of lunatics, a majority which changes in a few hours or a majority which is fixed—it is all one, majority is worshipped as of Divine Right.

Then comes someone who protests against the dogma, and all the fat is in the fire. There comes one who acts against it, and governs without regard to it, and men are as shocked as they were when the Divine Right of Kings was denied by the Popes of the 17th century.

Yes, the times have that one advantage, they are bestial and they stink, but they are amusing. The Immortals are having a good show for their money, and none of them is applauding more loudly or en-joying herself more in all that divine audience than my darling little Clio, with her spectacles and scant hair. She always was a favourite of mine.

The Gap

I SOMETIMES wonder whether the moral chaos into which Europe is falling will make the memories of better times—and especially our memories of travel—something so dim at last as to be obliterated. Certainly the generation now reaching manhood will be out of touch with the Europe we older people knew. Will man be able, forty years hence, to know that past at all? To realise it? That depends upon the duration of our present confusion. In this, the troubles of our time resemble a fire. If a fire can be put out fairly quickly the area of its devastation is mastered. The evil is circumscribed, limited and at last repaired. But if a fire smoulders on it not only spreads, but has a way of breaking out again here and there, beyond the boundaries of the original conflagration until at last it reduces everything to a heap of rubbish. So it may be with us.

I find it pathetic to notice in the midst of all our entanglements the steady stream of advertising still imploring us to visit this or that place, though, half the time, the place of which the illustration is given on the poster has either disappeared or is in the hands of mobs, or can be visited only at the peril of one's liberty: sometimes of one's life.

No doubt we of the West, and especially we who are fortunate enough to live in countries still quiet, exaggerate the peril and difficulties of travel to-day. I meet men from time to time who have returned from places I knew thirty years ago, and they speak of their journey as though it had been normal enough, going and coming. But then, these men are usually a good deal younger than myself. Only a minority of them can remember any considerable experience of European travel as it was before the outbreak of the Great War.

* * *

I shall always, in particular, regret having missed the Caucasus. I had my chance of seeing those great mountains in the year 1912, on my return from following the centenary celebrations of the Napoleonic campaign and studying Napoleon's retreat from Moscow.

It was open to me to return either directly via Berlin or, at a greater expense of time, by the South across the Caucasus to Georgia and so by the Black Sea. But I had been absent many weeks, and I thought it better to get home, saying to myself: "I have many years before me in which to visit the Caucasus with more elbow-room."

Nepios! I envisaged such a date as 'sixteen or 'seventeen; and when those years came round other things were toward, and there was no visiting the Caucasus in any easy fashion. Friends of mine have touched on the Euxine ports, but I know no one who has gone far inland along the range, whether from the Euxine or from the Caspian.

In the early nineties, friends of mine, living near my old constituency in Manchester, spoke to me often

of those hills and their majesty. These friends were
climbers who went there regularly for the sake of
their hobby. Have they been near the same places
during the last twenty years? I doubt it!

* * *

This cutting off of experience upon the surface of
the world is a great loss. It is the loss of a real wealth.
Seeing distant places—or, for that matter, any places
as yet unvisited—creates a sort of possession. One is
seized of such lands in a sort of spiritual tenure, and
no doubt they are, in a fashion, more our own than
any other lands. For the memories of them are undisturbed by accident nor are their images blurred by
repetition and continual change. Therefore, to have
missed a desired piece of travel is like missing a buried
treasure of which one knew the site and which one
proposed to unearth and enjoy, but which, in the
issue, was snatched away.

If this hiatus in the story of our civilisation is
sufficiently prolonged, it will leave behind it in our
general record a gap which will never be bridged,
and the younger generations will have no conception
of what my generation intimately and vividly knew.
For, mark you, there is no sufficient living experience
left to aid fancy on that dead past. In my childhood
of the seventies there was plenty of reminiscence by
the aged. My grandmother, in her childhood, had
crossed the Atlantic under sail, and could tell us
children clearly enough what that journey was. The
chief personage in the village where I was born could

speak to me of Waterloo. The news had reached his home when he was a boy, and in adolescence, he met many who had fought on that field. In all the books and on all the walls there was, of course, a crowd of illustrations from the older world before the railway and the steamship, but they were not mere pictures. They were inhabited by a lively spirit which had come down through a continuous civilisation, and there was no such complete gap in between as is now made by the years 1914-1918.

The transition from that older world—the world in which I was born—to the later years before the war, was bridged also by reminiscences of travel which my elders retained. The gentle tenor of life had not so greatly changed. The railway had transformed long voyages, but horse traffic still governed all local movement. Houses were still private. Visiting was announced, and leisurely. A County Town was a County Town, and the villages of Western Europe were still spiritually self-contained. The great towns and their new spirit had not yet invaded the countrysides. No doubt the new machines—particularly wireless and the cinema—were bound to brew a crop of new things. The internal-combustion engine had already arrived, and was bound to breed a further crop of still greater changes. Yet the spiritual continuity with the past would have stood the strain— but for the cataclysm of the great war. The life of Europe had been continuous. But how shall the lads growing into manhood thirty years hence understand, say, the Moscow of Tolstoy's time, or even the Paris of the Second Empire? What continuous lines of communication will they retain? None. All the vital links will have been broken. Their grandfathers have already become grotesque.

*   *   *

The conclusion is a grave one, giving matter for thought, not necessarily tragic, but profound. Were there present a fixed philosophy handed on from the past and generally accepted throughout European society to-day and throughout the New World which has proceeded from it, recovery would be certain. But there is none such—or perhaps it is truer to say that there is none such as yet firmly established, still less firmly recovered from the older days.

There is about this breach in our moral defences something like what happened nearly 600 years ago, when the Black Death swept over Western Europe. That catastrophe also divided the past from the future. It has been well called "The water shed of the middle ages." But so strong were then the traditions by which men held, that Europe, Western Europe, survived the shock. It was very much changed, but its personality survived. There did indeed come, after a sufficient lapse of time, certain belated effects which cut off the past and made of Christendom a new thing. Confused, but more vigorously alive than ever. That parallel may be at once instructive and consoling to us. It teaches us that even after the worst strains staggering Europe can find its feet again. It teaches us also that only after

the better part of a lifetime does the full effect of
any great blow—a major war or pestilence—begin to
be felt. It teaches us, therefore, that we must stand
by for greater moral changes to come in our society
than those which we to-day, the older of us, watch
with anxiety around us.

*   *   *

All this has led me very far away from the Caucasus,
and my regrets for that imagined and probably never-
to-be-enjoyed vision of great hills. But it was under
the influence of Caucasus—though far off—that
Medea lit the fire beneath her cauldron.

. . . when over Caucasus morning paled,
And through the dusk of dawn a broadening sea. . . .
Would that the Hull of Argo had not sailed!

Medea thus magically pretending to renew those
upon whom she practised her incantations, yet was
her magic unable to preserve those things which she
was asked to preserve.

Yes, it was under the memory of Caucasus, though
far away, that Medea brewed her broth. Let the thing
be a symbol, and let this recollecting of the Caucasus,
which I missed, promise some attempted renewal of
things that seem lost for ever.

But really, there is not very much to be hoped
under the sign of Medea. Is there?

The Test of Time

IT WAS the last performance of "Hamlet" at the Old Vic that moved me to consider for the hundredth time what innumerable men have considered throughout the ages. Since they have reached no sure conclusion, it is not likely that I shall. The thing thus continually considered, pondered upon, unsolved, is the effect of time upon making the name and glory of a poet.

That time is thus creative of fame and of endurance therein no one can doubt. The effect is right before us everywhere. It is manifest. We may often ask, upon contemporaries or even upon men of a lifetime ago, what stature they have reached, and whether their position is permanent. But upon older names we do not debate for we are all agreed. There is indeed a sort of itch for paradox and originality, which leads certain men to decry fantastically even the greatest names, as do those who have called Virgil "the greatest of the minor poets". It reminds me of an old acquaintance, now dead (himself a poet of sorts and too well-known while he lived), who would have it that John Milton was a windbag. But eccentrics may always be neglected where judgment is concerned. We all know that the great names are secure, and rightly secure, and we can see for ourselves that time has done it.

But *how* does time have this effect, and *why* should that factor in fame be at once essential and leisurely in action?

The rate of its effect differs vastly. With some reputations the growth is slow indeed. With others, more
surprisingly, it is so rapid as to seem extravagant.
For we say to ourselves, "Here is this man, now
seated among the stars. And yet he climbed to that
height at once, while all his peers had to wait so
long." There are poets who have been acclaimed at
their first accent, and some who were even within
their own life-times what they have ever since remained. Scholars assure me that this is true of
Sophocles. But even with these there was *some* element of time; there was a growth in recognition and
in common applause; and with far the greater part of
such men the process has been deliberate; there has
been a gradual unveiling and a gradual fixing of
fame, and of that which lies behind fame and is of
greater import than fame—the absolute value of the
verse.

* * *

Shakespeare is among the strongest of all examples.
It is difficult to gauge things not subject to measure-
ment. It is not easy to say "in such and such a generation the name of Shakespeare held such and such a
rank. In such and such a generation that rank was
this much higher." But it is certainly true of Shakespeare that the men who lived just after him had in
general, whatever their own excellence of ear and
taste, no such appreciation of the work done as had
those of the mid-eighteenth century; and it is surely
true that the men of 150 years ago did not put him
upon so exalted a level as we put him to-day.

Shakespeare's is of all historic reputations, I suppose, that which has grown most steadily, and one of those which has grown somewhat tardily. Time has done it; and we are as certain of what time has here done as we are of time's action upon some material thing, such as a tree, an effect testified to by our senses. No man can now effectively decry the very numerous and diverse triumphs of Shakespeare, or belittle him, any more than he can decry one of the great mountain ranges.

I remember a conversation held between a man of very high reputation among our contemporaries on the one hand, and the late Mr Gilbert Chesterton and myself on the other. This man maintained that Shakespeare was absurdly overrated, and gave as an example of his failure the insufficient construction of his plots. To this Mr Chesterton and myself each replied, in our various ways, that the glory of Shakespeare lay not in the construction of plots, but in the excellence of his poetry, whereat our interlocutor replied in his turn: "Oh! *Poetry!*" He put some scorn into his intonation of that word. Therein, I, for one, cannot agree with him; for, as it seems to me, to excel in poetry is, after holiness, the highest of human achievements.

*   *   *

Once more, why does time define and confirm such excellence? How does time work on this task? The answer is often given: "Because with the passing of time the adventitious drops out, is forgotten, loses importance, and only the essential interests, those which are common to all mankind, remain." Now I cannot help believing that this answer, which has been so universally given, especially during the last century, is at fault. For the greatness of verse does not lie in its subject but in its manner. The soul of verse is form. Men think that what is affirmed in such and such a great line appeals to them by its truth. That is—by its correspondence with experience. But indeed it is not so. The great verse strikes not by wisdom but by magic. Poetry lies in magic. That which purports to be poetry but fails in magic has missed its aim, and is commonly, as poetry, worthless. When Shakespeare wrote: "The Glimpses of the Moon," he rang the bell—and the operative word is "Glimpses". If he had written "Intermittent Appearances," he would have spoilt the dish.

*   *   *

Now because poetry is magic the effect of time upon it may be compared to the washing of pay-dirt (as I used to hear it called by my seniors in California before the world grew old). Pay-dirt meant the earth that was washed for its residuum of gold. The gold fell of its own weight, the dross was carried away; and here would seem to be a parallel to what time does with verse. For the effect of verse is confirmed by repetition and multitudinous appreciation. The individual who has been struck to the heart by one phrase may at first be uncertain of his appreciation; but the thing returns to him when his mood has changed, when it is blurred by fatigue, or weakened by frequent use or degraded by inferior circumstance; and each time, as that verse returns, it gives witness to itself making the recipient increasingly sure that his first judgment was right. Now if that is true of the effect of time upon an individual appreciation, it is far more profoundly and widely true of the effect of time upon general appreciation: "What! You too felt that verbal stab? Then surely I was not deceived in my reception of it!" And this man and that other, and yet a third, nods and agrees. "Minds of different mould acting in most varied circumstance all converge on this, do they? Why then we must between us all be right enough; we may continue to murmur 'The Glimpses of the Moon'."

On the Immediate Past

WE ALL owe a debt of gratitude to the Immediate Past.

I mean by Immediate Past the generation before our own and just overlapping into our own: the generation which was mature when we were very young: the generation of our parents, if we were born late in their lives, or of our grandparents—but not of grandparents born so long ago as to become picturesque and venerable.

We owe the Immediate Past gratitude in the first place (obviously) because it gave us the gift of life. It is our progenitor; and if there is anyone so lost to common sense as to think existence is in itself an evil, I cannot argue with him here. But we owe the Immediate Past special gratitude in other and particular ways, one of which is the fun which it affords, especially in the way of dressing. I fancy the Immediate Past in our own case is peculiarly ridiculous, more ridiculous than the Immediate Past ever was before.

The men of the early nineteenth century hardly thought the graces of the mid-eighteenth century ridiculous. They may have thought them finicking and silly, but they could hardly have thought them merely comic. They could not have thought the style of Louis XV grotesque. But we certainly find the dresses and the coats and trousers, even the men's hats of the Immediate Past, grotesque, and the one that takes the prize is the billycock or bowler of that period. We think our own billycocks (or bowler hats) natural only because we are used to them, but the billycocks which you see on the heads of the toffs in the illustrations which Millais and others drew for reproduction in wood, and to portray the characters of Trollope, strike one like a blow.

*　　*　　*

I have often meditated on this important theme. I think I have got to the root of the matter. It is the absurd brim that does it. The brim of the billycock of the early seventies is something quite out of nature. The marvel is how the men of that day managed to catch hold of it at all when they did what some called "raising their hats".

The top hat of the eighties, which I remember well, was not without dignity. It shone, and all shining things command a certain measure of worship. But the stove-pipe hat, its immediate predecessor, was a scream and remains a scream. That again you may study in the older wood-cuts, and study with profit: which reminds me of a favourite question, "What will happen to the top hat?"

It is now only used on special ceremonial occasions: occasions such that it cannot be worn upon the head, save for a few moments. It is used in weddings, where it stands upside down on a pew, or is carried awkwardly in the hand. It is used at funerals. I seem to have read somewhere that it is still used in the House of Commons (but I will not swear to that). It is used at certain social functions of the collective sort among the wealthy; but bar these uses and it is no longer used at all. Yet it survives. It is something remaining so far immortal out of the very mortal Immediate Past. Perhaps it will be retained for centuries, like the coronet or the sword: an uneasy thought, but that is the common fate of things which have come to have only a rare and ceremonial use.

We should also be grateful to the Immediate Past, not only for the fun it affords us, but for the opportunity it gives us for self-praise, complacency, vanity and all the rest of the pleasant human faults. It is in contemplating the Immediate Past that we see how much better we are than those people. As a fact we are much worse. But we notice the things in which they lived either less comfortably than we do, or less neatly, or (for what that may be worth), less expeditiously. We do not note the things in which they manifestly excelled us—as, for instance, wine buckets. I myself can just remember the time when wine buckets were deep enough to cool wine: that is, when they still fulfilled their function. To-day they are used to advertise to the company in the eating house that certain of the guests are drinking champagne. This dazzling achievement could not be advertised by the old wine bucket, for it was too deep and gave you no hint as to what was within. But the modern wine bucket (not being designed to cool wine but to show the gilt paper covering the neck of the bottle), advertises the gooseberry and thereby sheds a triple glory on the consumer, the provider and the neighbour—

who is given thereby a sensation of magnificence and marble halls.

*   *   *

We ought, of course, to be grateful to the Immediate Past also for models which, if we are wise enough to follow them, would make our own lives less intolerable; but the trouble is that we never copy these models and most of us never even see them.

Thus the Immediate Past had far more comfortable chairs, far more comfortable beds, far more subdued light, and if you cease to care for none of these things, if you are a Galileo for physical comfort, at least you will admit that in one thing the Immediate Past has a model for us: not only the light but the conversation was subdued. It was the fashion in those days to modulate speech and to keep what you were saying to the little circle in which it was said. There was no bawling and no screaming, and there was no music at public meals, or, at any rate, very little, save occasional music at special dinners, mainly consisting of good songs, well rendered. But well-bred conversation and subdued tone in speech cannot be recovered, because the models are no longer with us. There is no one to copy. And if we did recover that older manner people would ask us to say it again because they did not catch it. The Immediate Past gave us a good deal of bad art, but no tomfoolery, pretending to be art. It gave us some very fine verse indeed, and not a little fine prose, and we can certainly show our gratitude for *that*, though we do not. For I take it that if a certain amount of the good verse is still read, hardly any of the good prose is. Some of the good rhetoric is read; but rhetoric, however good, is not prose, though it is often called prose and singled out for praise as prose.

*   *   *

I was going to say that we ought to be grateful to the Immediate Past for its discoveries. But even as I approached that laudation I was struck cold at the heart. Are these discoveries things for which we ought to be grateful? I fear not! We might have used them so that they should have been of universal benefit— but we have not so used them. You will, on a survey, find very few such discoveries of which you can say, "This has brought a blessing without too evil an effect."

Yet, take it all in all, the Immediate Past has the advantage over us that in the main we *can* be grateful to it, and are beginning to admire it. Now we can be quite certain of this, that no one will be grateful to *us* when *we* become the Immediate Past, and of admiration we certainly shall receive none at all— only indifference and hate.

On Portraits in History

It is a fortunate thing that photography did not exist in the days when history was really interesting. Those who wanted to perpetuate their own features, or the features of people prominent in their family, had to rely upon human talent, and this was exercised with a real care to make a portrait as like as possible to the person it portrayed. The work was nearly always finished with care: for it is significant that all this new-fangled stuff of half-done sketchy work (it calls itself by a dozen eccentric names) began to come in just about the time when photography was getting common. A photograph will, indeed, now and then give a most living portrait; but it is purely haphazard, and usually a snapshot which nobody took care about or a face which is only a detail in a group. There is plenty of real portraiture to-day, pictures of people drawn by the human hand, and, therefore, having passed through a human mind, and a mind working with a special intention of making a faithful record. But for the past we have to rely entirely upon such, and I say again it is fortunate that we are left with no alternative. For though a picture done by the human hand suffers from the personal factor, yet at least we do get a living thing.

You can never get a sufficient grasp of a character long dead unless you see it exemplified by a painting, a drawing or a bust. I find in my own little sphere that if I am writing about an historical character and cannot get hold of a contemporary representation, my conclusion remains vague. A literary description may give substance to the image one tries to make in one's mind. For instance, when we are told that Charlemagne had a squeaky voice and was paunchy, though tall, it helps one to grasp him in some degree. But what a different thing it would be if we had the man himself on canvas or in stone as we should have if he had lived six hundred years later!

*   *   *

It is a pity that modern people have thought it their duty to set up monuments of the great dead of whom they have no pictorial or sculptural evidence. Such a habit warps history badly. Witness the monstrous Alfreds on more than one market-place in South England. Also one particular extravagance to which I often return: the Victorian gentleman on horseback who prances in front of the Houses of Parliament at Westminster and is called Richard the First of England, Plantagenet.

It is, indeed, with the Plantagenets that I feel most acutely the poverty of illustration by effigy. There is no group of men more fascinating to consider than those fierce fellows who had a demon for their ancestress (she used to turn into a winged dragon and fly out of the window at night) and who had about them the energy of the Great Cats; the men who carried on the blood of Fulk and Melisande. Of course, there are the sculptures on the tombs at Fontrevault; but though they are striking they are still too primitive.

One gets a fairly good idea of those stocky bullet-headed Frenchmen, Frenchmen of the Northern sort, of the sort that made the type of William the Conqueror, when one looks on those faces at Fontrevault. But how I wish one could have had the same men put before one by Houdin or by the intense sculptors of the fourteenth and fifteenth centuries. In particular would I desire to see Henry the Second of England as he was and especially if the artist had hinted at his fits of rage. It was not for nothing that the Angevins put themselves under the patronage of the leopard. Nor was he, or rather they (for there were three leopards) a smooth sinuous beast. He had fire in him and he expressed it by thrusting out his tongue extravagantly. Yet of all the Angevins the one I should really like to know by portraiture, the one we certainly know most imperfectly by his effigy, is John.

John of England stands all by himself. Even as his family went he was especially ferocious, especially brave and tempestuous. His cruelty was dynamic. So was his military talent. And he managed to put more into his short and I am afraid, deservedly unpopular life, than any other of his line. Even if he had lived another few weeks he would not have reached fifty. He was well hated and he certainly cared nothing for the hatred of any man. Yet with luck he might have been one of the great heroes. He had a flame in him. It has always seemed to me that he was a worthy last antagonist for the Capetians in that duel from which the Plantagenets never fully recovered. But talking of the French kings, the sculpture of Philip le Bel

which is, I think, in the Gallery of the Kings at
Rheims, is the most striking thing of the kind I
know. It may be doubted, of course, whether it is
really Philip le Bel, though that is presumable. But
tradition makes it so and certainly the face is consonant with what we know of the man. There is a
cold intensity about it and a will, not without evil,
which is worthy of the trial of the Templars, and the
awful scene on the little island in the Seine, just
beyond the palace, where the burning was.

*   *   *

The men of the sixteenth and seventeenth centuries
were the most fortunate in their message to posterity.
For they lived at a time when the creative power of
portraiture was at its highest. After that it declined;
and declined, I think, as much as for any other cause,
from the use of the wig. Some few faces are strong
enough to carry the wig without losing themselves in
a sort of uniformity. That was certainly true of Louis
XIV's face. But the greater part of them are more
wig than man. And when they were without their
wigs and got themselves painted with a sort of hand-
kerchief round their shaven heads, they cut no sufficient figure. I always find something weak about
human expression when it is crowned thus.

Men may say that women were fortunate in that
they escaped the wig, or at least escaped the open
admission of it. But then for some reason or other
the paintings and drawings and busts representing
women hardly ever strike one so forcibly as do those

representing men. There is indeed one sculpture of a woman's face in marble which holds depths upon depths of character, of experience, of suffering and a sort of spiritual maturity. It is presumably Italian work, but we have the good fortune to possess it here in this country. No one knows who did it and no one knows whom it represents. That is just as well.

The Despot and the Arts

THERE IS in Europe now a strong tendency to what its supporters call "totalitarian government". The old-fashioned name for that kind of thing was despotism, and perhaps it is better to keep to the old title because everybody knows what it means. If these despotic governments remain powerful, and still more if their system spreads, the effects on the arts will certainly be marked, particularly upon the literary arts, because it is by these that men express themselves and by these they are moved to various political and other emotions.

What effect will the despot have upon the fortunes of the writing man and his audience? What effect will he have in particular upon the dramatist and his audience? What effect will he have upon the stage? The first answer that would be given to such a question by anyone brought up under the old Liberal traditions of Europe would be that despotism is fatal to art of all kinds. The essence (we should be told) of art is freedom—because any art being the self-expression of the artist, if he is constrained in any way his activity will be maimed. But the supporters of the new despotic form of government in Europe deny the value of this argument under modern conditions. What they say is that under modern conditions art is debased by two things, the taste of the mob, and what is closely associated with that, the power of great sums of money. They would say that art in a highly

developed civilisation is always subject to restrictions
and it is simply a choice of what kind of restriction
you prefer. Even in the most liberal state and one
with the highest public taste there is a certain amount
of censorship, especially upon stage plays, and there
must be such, otherwise there would be no limit to
the obscenity and blasphemy which might be put
before the people, to the destruction of society.

Violent extremes always attract by novelty and the
acuteness of sensation which they provide for the
moment. The tendency therefore if there were no
censorship of stage plays would be for the most disgusting and degrading extremes of violent emotion
to be pandered to.

But (say those who now support despotic government) to-day there is no practical question of censorship by public good taste, for public good taste has
disappeared. The proletarian herds of our modern
industrial cities will either demand the worst or be
given the worst by their few plutocratic masters. It
is better for them and for the world that limits should
be chosen and imposed by men who, being all powerful, cannot be bought and cannot be deceived.

They have another argument from history which
is a very powerful one. It is simply this: that the best
work in every department of art, and particularly in
dramatic art, has been done under strong central
governments. There have been exceptions to the
contrary. But that has been the rule. There is no
good art without a patron, and when an all powerful
monarch is the chief patron art should naturally be

at its best. One spirit acting with intensity and sum-
marising the energies of the whole community inspires all that is done. Florence was at its best under
the Medicis. French drama was at its highest under
Louis XIV—and so on.

To this the other side reply: "None of the old
central governments acted with the complete despotism of the modern centralised governments. These
have certainly killed political expression in the press
and the art of political discussion; their strength is so
absolute and their influence so universal that the same
deadening must appear in whatever else they affect
and particularly will that loss of vitality be apparent
in the drama".

But the new despotic governments answer this by
saying that you can actually see them at work and
discover that they have no such evil effects. The only
thing (they say) which is in practice prohibited is
something which is nearly always productive of bad
dramatic work, and that is revolutionary doctrine:
attack upon authority. If you do not attack the execu-
tive of the state your art will be left perfectly free.
What is more, it will be rescued from the vulgarity
and decline which invariably accompany the control
of the state by mere wealth. To-day in all countries
boasting of freedom, in all large countries at any
rate, capitalism has become completely master. Now
the despot has for his chief task the fighting of the
money power. Napoleon put it in one of his innumerable terse and striking judgments: "The only instru-

ment mankind has ever discovered for defeating the money power is monarchy."

It is indeed principally upon this plea of reversing and emending the increasing evil results of capitalism that the modern despots have seized upon power. Whether they call themselves openly Communists as at Moscow or rather Nationalists as at Berlin and at Rome, the mass support they get—and it is very solid and looks like being enduring—comes from the popular feeling that they do at any rate master the mere power of gold.

It is the excesses of Capitalism which have produced the modern despotic governments, and hitherto we can see for ourselves (say their supporters) that the system works well, fills society with most active life and therefore must of its nature inspire the arts.

You meet men all over Europe, men at once intelligent and enthusiastic who will tell you that the revival of the arts, and with them of the drama must come to-day and can only come to-day from society under absolute centralised government. These men talk everywhere of the new world which is being born. They associate this new world with the presence of irresistible central government under a leader or leaders whose function it is to incarnate all the society which they control. In that new world art will, like everything else, be new-born. We shall have a Renaissance after the deserved breakdown of 19th century capitalism, and in that Renaissance we shall find glories which we could not have dreamt of in the old unhappy state of things where most men were driven by competition to a life of such grinding anxiety, and usually of poverty as well, that there could be no room for art. When it is pointed out to them that the new despotic states have as a fact produced very little worth seeing or reading, and that in particular the drama has been sterile, they answer that we must give the new experiment more time, and that anyhow its productions are not below the very low standard of the recent past.

There is another argument. The despotic state has at its disposal for the patronage of the arts unlimited funds. To-day the painter for instance is dependent upon the caprice of a few individual rich men, most of whom have become rich by the exercise of cunning or worse, and are cast in a mould fatal to the understanding of art in any form. This is less true of the drama, but it is largely true of the drama also, and certainly of that press by which the drama is judged and advertised.

Now all these arguments in favour of the novel experiment in despotism which we see all around us in Europe (and which is manifestly growing in power) must be appreciated if we are to understand the virtues as well as the errors which would appear before us in the near future. The arguments in favour of despotism are weak from the moral side; they are not very strong upon the political side, but on the economic side they are formidable and on the aesthetic side they are strongest of all.

But even on the aesthetic side there is one under-lying weakness which the supporters of despotism never face. It may be very simply stated and has been stated in the fullest clarity by every great thinker on politics and art who has attempted to teach mankind during the last three thousand years of Western civilisation.

It is simply this. That whether a despotism be of good or bad effect in any department, but particularly in art, depends upon the despot, his philosophy and his ability.

From this there flows a conclusion upon the new despotic experiment proceeding so rapidly in the Old World and spreading over so widely extended a field, which conclusion no public man seems as yet to have voiced. The conclusion is this, that despotic governments will very soon prove to be of the most varied kind. Despotism will not make for a universal type: quite the other way. It will make for very different results indeed according to the difference between the despots themselves and the material upon which they work.

Anyone can see for himself, for instance, the strong contrast between the effect of Fascism in Italy upon the arts—especially upon architecture—and the effect of the Nazi despotism in Prussianised Germany. Modern Italian building is majestic and modern planning in Italy of cities and their approaches is admirable. Nazi Prussianized Germany is even more despotic than Fascist Italy, but its public work is deplorable. It builds fine great roads which necessitate fine great bridges, and the bridges are as ugly as sin. It puts up huge buildings which are an eyesore, and when it ventures upon initiating a dramatic expression—such as the Hindenburg Funeral—it lapses into ridiculous melodrama, whereas Fascist Italy produces pageants of unforgettable splendour.

What the strange Moscow despotism does in the way of art I cannot judge, for I have not seen it at work. So far as pictures are any guide it seems to revel in the offensive, and if it has produced any drama worth seeing I can only say that we have had no echo in the rest of Europe.

This general conclusion that despotic government as it increases its area of action will breed strongly contrasting diversities of artistic experience has a very important political and social side to it. Those despotisms which are inspired by a strong artistic sense may well become models even for the societies which still retain institutions nominally free.

The Nazi blunders in art, the Communist offensiveness therein, would move no foreigner to copy them, except perhaps from pure snobbishness, the desire to do what is novel merely because it is novel: the worst, because the most irrational of all criteria. But any modern society may be proud to produce, if they can be produced, under conditions of a general voting, parliaments, millionaire newspaper owners and the rest, such sights as modern Fascist Italy can show.

I do not think that those inhabiting countries still attached to Liberal formulae (such as Ireland, England and France, Belgium and Holland) will easily fall under despotic forms of government. There is something so well established in their civic traditions that unlimited and absolute power in one centre is too repugnant to them to be adopted. Moreover they have never fallen as yet into such a chaos as the German Reich suffered after the War, or the social system of Italy before the Fascist Revolution. They have less motive for establishing despotism than men had in the Reich or in Italy, and they are less suited to obeying a despotism. But I do think that in the arts, and ultimately in drama as in all the other arts, a despotism which proves itself successful in the exhibition through art of beauty and majesty may easily become a model of the nations still possessing something of the old Liberal tone. I think it possible that a despotism guided by high taste and rewarding true artistic genius may rescue societies of other political type from artistic chaos.

On Euphemism

THE EUPHEMISM is a little creature deserving the closest attention. Its origin is always of interest, its youth and early growth of still greater interest, its struggle to maturity absorbing. Even when it has worn smooth in age and become a commonplace it is still a much better subject of study than the contemporaries of its youth might imagine. The Euphemism as a species is probably as old as human speech: and how old that is nobody knows, least of all the philologists. The Euphemism is born of that social sense without which man would not be man, and because it is so true a child of that sense it reflects from every facet characters of *Homo Civis,* Man the Citizen.

The Euphemism is a recognition by man of man's own imperfection, and at the same time a recognition by man that he belongs to better things. It is play acting, but none the worse for that. It is a false word substituted for the true word in order to soften the shock of reality.

A man stands on a platform. He is about to address a packed audience of Swindlers, Cowards, Bounders, Painted Harridans and Trulls. He opens his mouth to address them. What does he say? He says: "Ladies and gentlemen." Human language should be packed with Euphemisms. It is, indeed, proof that man was meant to live with his fellows, and proof also of how difficult it is for man to carry on that task without inordinate friction. It testifies also to the ingenuity of man himself, for we must note that the Euphemism ninety-nine times out of a hundred rises up from the masses; it has no one author, or if it has, that author is rarely known.

*   *   *

Take the commonest of the Euphemisms, the use of the second or third person in the place of the first. We say "You" instead of "Thou" because (Heaven knows how long ago!) it was thought more polite to pretend that the person addressed was too grand to be treated as a mere individual. He might not be a monarch, but it was only decent to give him the title of one. It is very pretty to see that in the transition towards the Dark Ages both the second person plural and the third person singular came into use for courteous address, and we keep up the habit to this day for the better conduct of human affairs. We write to an ambassador, "Your Excellency will hardly have failed to observe," where brute nature would have written "Don't sham ignorance." It is all to the good so to soften the edges of life. But, in connection with this useful and honourable human habit, remark that the Euphemism sometimes avenges itself. When it finds it is being overworked it revives with added force an original simple use which it was supposed to supplant. Thus the French express both insult and affection by saying "Thou" instead of "You", and in English we use "Thou" for adoration.

The Euphemism is sometimes killed at birth and

often killed in early youth. The wealthy and the powerful are always suspicious of it. A new Euphemism is nearly always Middle Class; usually it has to fight hard to get accepted. I could quote half a dozen which I have seen in my own lifetime either done to death or thrust down into the lower ranks of society to which they have, ever since their fall, been inexorably condemned. The use of "homely" as a Euphemism for ugly is an example in point; others, far more striking, I forbear to record through the respect I owe you.

Among Euphemisms thus ruthlessly exiled from the great world, never to re-enter it, are "mansion" and "approach". Both of them were originally of a very roundabout grandeur. Mansion (which is *mansio*) simply meant the place where you stop, and Approach was just approach; the way by which you got near to a place. But hardly had they taken on the air of grandeur when the wealthier classes came out against them to do battle and thrust them back into obscurity. But in doing so they again transformed them. Mansion became one of fifty ways of saying (in the plural) a town flat, while Approach after lingering painfully, licking its wounds for half a century, died—round about the seventies or eighties I think. At any rate, it is well dead now. We know "Drive" or "Avenue," but "Approach" is forgotten.

"Villa" is another glorious specimen. A "Villa" was a country estate of the Roman rich; a village community with the Lord's Great House in the midst. The word was then borrowed to save the face of the

suburbs. Now it has a disdainful sound. You may
hear a rich woman say of some habitation she
despises: "Oh! no! nothing of that sort! Just a villa."

*   *   *

It is sadly true of the Euphemism that when it has
got itself well rooted and established it dies in another way: not by losing its body, but by losing its
soul. It becomes a commonplace word like any other.
We come to use it straightforwardly, as though it had
never been a Euphemism at all. A Judge in Cham-
bers, Chamber music, the Upper Chamber, all the
hundred uses of that word, come from the late Latin
for a vault. It was thought more polite to allude to a
man's room as his "vaults" because the great Roman
palaces would be vaulted where the little Roman
houses had plain flat floors and roofs. When you talk
of the "camber" of the road, you are using the same
word but in quite another sense. And, what is amusing, you talk of the camera in photography with no
sort of relation to any vault at all, nor even to any
house but a box.

Euphemisms grow unnaturally and dangerously by
competition, very much as do advertisements, super-
latives, and words of emphasis. One Euphemism will
supplant another in a few years and then be destroyed
again in its turn, like the outlaw of the Nemi wood by
a supplanter. A neat case of this which has happened
almost within a lifetime is the Euphemism for madhouse. A madhouse is something unpleasant; so, man
being a social animal, he must give it a name pleas-

anter than the true one. He began early by calling it
a Bethlehem, from a charitable foundation dedicated
to the Nativity and coming to function as a refuge
for the afflicted. Hence Bedlam. When Bedlam had
ceased to be even tolerably polite, we invented asylum. Asylum is a very beautiful word. It should by
rights be full of repose and peace, for it means a secure refuge. But Asylum wore thin in less than a century. We have got by now to "Mental Hospital"; and
it is a sad tribute to the divine intelligence of man
that "mental" already means with the poor (and perhaps in time will mean with the rich) a person of
distracted mind. What Euphemism will men use when
they have grown frightened of "Mental Hospital"?

*   *   *

We never know what the next Euphemism will be.
It comes up out of the depths and steals upon us un-
awares. I doubt whether a locution which is a favourite with the leisured English will ever take final root,
though I confess I am very fond of it myself because
it always reminds me of that high genius in whose
writings I first found it: P. G. Wodehouse. I mean,
the term "loony-bin". It is admirable, it is first-rate,
therefore it will go down the dark way which all the
best things of this world must tread; the road to oblivion: the unreturning way. Perhaps it will not die
in my time, but if it does I shall mourn it sincerely.

And so much for Euphemism. Do not attempt to
live without it in a fit of straightforwardness, for if
you do you will pass an unhappy manhood and a
lonely old age. Not that I care.

On Boasting

IF IT be true that our civilization is in decline—I am pretty certain it is—one symptom of the decline must be a certain loss of refinement in the arts. When a civilization is running down the things which it used to do with exactitude and delicacy combined (and with that power of concealing effort which is the supreme test) are done more openly, more crudely, and not so thoroughly. This is true today of a very great number of things, and particularly I notice a lamentable falling-off in the art of boasting.

Boasting is not without its uses. We must not lightly condemn it. The individual who "gives himself value" is making himself a person well worth having, for with boasting as with all other forms of falsehood something remains, something sticks. The man who tells you at great length and with a certain manly modesty the wonderful things he has done in the hunting of wild beasts, may not in fact have fired a shot in his life at anything more dangerous than a rabbit if he is poor, or a pheasant if he is rich, but you know that he has travelled, and you cannot help forming pictures in your mind as he carries on with his tale. However much of these pictures you reject, the image remains with you. You will say, "Joe is intolerable with all those stories of his about his tiger hunting in India!" You are prepared to hear that he has exaggerated. But you would be startled to hear that there was not a word of truth in the whole business.

The boaster then does procure credit to himself in a certain degree, and usually he procures it in a high degree; and if that is true of individual boasting it is especially true of collective boasting, which is the commoner form, and indeed is almost universal.

The collective boaster is one who cracks up the deeds and qualities of his family, his school, his county, and especially his nation. The boaster born is led by every inducement to this collective form. When it is applied to the whole nation it is thought patriotic, and no one blames it. When it is applied to a social class, to an occupation, to a school or college at which the boaster suffered in youth, there is a sort of lesser patriotism in play which is also thought amiable by one's fellow-men. The collective boaster also strengthens the organism which he belauds. The individual boaster strengthens himself to some extent but perilously; the collective boaster can go much further without provoking any action, and at the same time he is safely strengthening himself, for his hearers cannot but think, "This fellow must have something in him if he were a member of so great a thing!"

Thus a man the other day, a learned historian, began a letter to the newspapers with the words, "An example of our political wisdom is the recruitment of the House of Lords." He not only strengthened the House of Lords (though that institution stood in no need of his help); he not only strengthened his nation in the opinion of those who read him; but he strengthened himself. The implication was that a nation so stuffed with political wisdom as to produce the average peer, must have communicated much of its wisdom to a son so favoured as to hold an official position in a national university. In future you may read this academic person's history and feel strongly tempted to think it rubbish, until you are checked by remembering that he comes of a race packed with political wisdom. So when he says, for instance, "Anne Boleyn had nothing to do with the divorce of Henry VIII, she was but a side issue in the affair," you comment within yourself, "To an ignorant man like me that sounds nonsense; but since Professor So-and-So says it, there must be something in it, because he enjoys that great national inheritance, Political Wisdom."

Boasting has this further advantage, that it makes the boaster genuinely better contented with himself and the world. It promotes, if I may use the metaphor, spiritual digestion. It is noticed that men who are very anxious about their souls often have bad digestions; men quite certain of their souls should therefore presumably have good digestions. I will ask one of them some day, for I am acquainted with a great number: yes, I will ask him if it is not so, but indeed I am sure it is so, from the happy contented expression of this breed.

How do we know that the art of boasting is in decline? How can we measure its increasing degree of crudity? I think by the increasing degree of directness in manner. Old-fashioned boasting was indirect and the really best bred sort was so indirect that you hardly knew it for boasting until it had done its work. For instance, you would hear a story of heroism at sea. The story was repeated in many a book and newspaper; it became a myth. Doubtless it gave a false effect and was largely intended to give a false effect, but that false effect was not produced by beginning, "There are few finer examples of our sailors' courage . . ." It began by giving a date, describing the weather, naming the ship and her master, and then going through the details of the affair, all very exciting and accurate, and omitting pretty well anything that would read unfavourably. A subtler form than direct narrative and omission of disagreeables is the introduction of favourable comparisons from outside. Thus you would say that this particular tale of heroism reminded one very much of the action of certain foreigners in the same circumstances. By this you enhance the effect of your boasting, because the reader says, "This man is impartial: I cannot refuse to accept what he says about his own people since he is willing to give almost as much credit to others."

Again, it is a refined, a civilized form of boasting, to mix it with a proper dose of affection. For instance, you want to impress your audience with the wealth of your family and the consequent magnitude of the palace (or country house, as it is called) which it built for itself just after it had first captured the swag. You bring into all you say a tone of the love you bear to the old place; your reminiscences of childhood; your tenderness for its every detail: the blue drawing-room, the little drawing-room, the ballroom, your father's study, and that fine old table which you have always heard came from the Walpoles (though it is true you do not pretend to have proof of that—it is only a family tradition), the lovely mellow light on the old brick of the big kitchen garden, the stables, which are in the manner of Sir Christopher Wren, the quaint lodges, the skill with which your great-grandfather disguised these last in the Gothic manner of the early nineteenth-century—and this you gently ridicule. Then there is the view over the lake, which was not used at first as a lake but was a millpond until a little after the '45, and that magnificent changing outline of Ben Machlin, or Pen-y-Gwilt, or Mt. Haberdash, or whatever it is. Nor will you fail to point out that the place is happily so far removed from Badleigh Abbey as not to be overshadowed and dwarfed by that neighbourhood. It will go hard if before this kind of thing is over the full effect of the boasting has not soaked in.

There was also in my youth that most excellently subtle form of boasting which may be called the elliptical. You left out the most important point which everybody knew, and the implication was that you were so grand (or your people, or your ancestors, or whatever it was you were talking about were so grand) that this point didn't matter. The most perfect form of elliptical boasting (which is saying nothing at all) has almost gone out. It survives in only one department I think—silence about titles.

And so much for boasting. And one happy note to end with. Fierce blatant boasting of great deeds *by the man who has actually done them* is on the increase. It was quite new only a few years ago. It is splendid fun, and I hope to see it increase. It may be called "integral boasting": and I do hope that no one will rule out this kind of boasting on the plea that there is no true boasting without falsehood.

On Speaking Too Soon

TELLING THE news, like telling any kind of truth, is dangerous and cannot be unlimited. Obviously dangerous to the man who tells the truth, but dangerous also to the community he addresses. The only practical debate in the matter is on the degree of falsehood that ought to be admitted in order that the truth shall be of value. We are all agreed that without a little falsehood life would be impossible. Gold cannot be worked without an alloy, it is not stiff enough.

The contention advanced by those of us who insist on telling certain truths and publishing certain news which the official Press does not mention, is that the measure of falsehood has become too great for the good of the community. More truth ought to be told, especially on matters concerning the good of the State in foreign and Imperial affairs—and even on domestic affairs in some degree.

But there is another aspect to the problem: the truth is not only suppressed, it is often simply unknown, and the proportionate value of various truths still less known. It is very difficult to get the owner of a London newspaper to understand, for instance, the difference between Basque and Catalan in the present Spanish struggle; but it is still more difficult to make him understand the importance of Basque and Catalan in the settlement that will follow on the civil war. Until lately it was even difficult to make either the few wealthy owners of the newspapers or any appreciable number of their readers grasp the importance of the Spanish civil war at all. Lately that defect has been remedied in some degree; people are beginning to understand that the issue between Communism and tradition in Spain will powerfully affect the rest of Europe.

There is yet another aspect of the problem, the time at which a truth should be told in a matter of debate. If you tell a truth too soon it will almost certainly be neglected, for two reasons; first of all it would seem to have no interest at the moment; and second, it will be forgotten before its application can be experienced. This gives to the telling of truth too soon a character of futility. There is a waste of effort, with no practical result. Whoever has told the truth too soon can boast later on and cry, "I told you so!" and that may be a consolation to his vanity, but it is no use at all to the public in whose service presumably the truth was told.

There were a good many people—more than twenty, perhaps a hundred—in a position to make themselves heard, who saw as early as 1911 that the Great War was likely to break out in 1914 or thereabouts. Some of them said as much, but it led to no adequate preparation. There were plenty of people to tell their fellow-citizens forty years ago that the collection of rents from the Irish in order to pay usury to the Banks in London could not endure, that the various Land Acts were only palliatives and that in the long run there would be an explosion.

There were even quite a respectable number who told us when the burden had been shifted by the Wyndham Land Act, that the payment of annuity tribute to England could not be permanent. But even now they are not listened to, in spite of the event.

Take the run of forecasts based upon sufficient knowledge and judgment and you will find that much the greater part are forgotten, or remembered too late. At the moment of their appearance they fell flat. They do no useful work. For instance, it is now some thirty years since quite a large number of men with experience of Islam began to say that Islam would not remain permanently disarmed; that the power of the Moslem world would re-arise. But even now, with the symptoms of the thing on every side, the impression of it is very confused and faint.

Nevertheless speaking too soon is worth while. If it is futile in 99 cases out of 100 it does have some practical effect in the hundredth case. Men who knew Poland, for instance, said immediately after the Armistice that the future of that country was assured. Nearly everyone in this country took it for granted that Poland would not survive. But the people who knew Poland were of course right, for though ignorance may make a lucky guess by mistake, it does not often do so. The men who said Poland would endure spoke five or six years too soon, but they were remembered when the event began to confirm their judgment. And it was in part due to their rehabilitation that our general attitude towards the Polish case changed.

After all, the only person who suffers by telling the truth too soon is the man who tells it; and he does not suffer much, he only suffers from neglect and contempt. He does not suffer nearly as much as a man who tells an unpleasant truth, which everybody knows to be true but which everybody wants to conceal. Indeed, take it all round, telling the truth too soon would seem to be not only one of the wisest forms of telling the truth but one of the most useful, for if it only has practical effect once in a hundred times, that is a pretty high rate of efficiency.

On Books

FEAR NOTHING. I do not propose to write on what is inside books. Nothing shall persuade me to do so! Of all fatiguing, futile, empty trades, the worst, I suppose, is writing about writing.

Writing itself is a bad enough trade, rightly held up to ridicule and contempt by the greater part of mankind, and especially by those who do real work, ploughing, riding, sailing—or even walking about. It is a sound instinct in men to feel this distrust and contempt for writing; and as for writing about writing, why, it is writing squared; it is writing to the second power, in which the original evil is concentrated. Such writing on writing is to mere writing what those abominable chemical meat extracts are to common soup. There is even, I am told, a third degree of horror. Writing about what other people have written about writing: "Lives of the Critics," "Good English," "Essays on Sainte Beuve"—things of that sort. Good Lord, deliver us!

No, I am not concerned with what is inside books. From that I turn my mind away with horror. I am concerned with books as material objects. They have not been sufficiently considered in that light—"from that angle," as modern people say—and yet they are of vast interest "from that angle."

There is your book as missile, for instance, a thing of poignant interest from no matter what angle you receive it: on your chin, your cheekbone, or your eye.

There is your book as support or heightener. For this purpose Encyclopaedias are of high merit, and Mr E. V. Lucas—in a work that shall never die, or rather will certainly resurrect, his work of thirty years ago on *The Times* edition of the *Encyclopaedia Britannica*—pointed out of what real value those huge books are in helping baby to sit up at table.

Then there is your book as an architectural unit (which is a nice long name for a brick or a stone). Many a man in very early youth has found his father's library useful for building cromlechs or little caves, and I have known them used by the young of military mind to do duty as soldiers, or the *simulacra* thereof. A row of books, more or less the same size, stood up on end and placed about half a height apart, makes a perfect file. You push the *chef de file*, he falls against his neighbour, he against the next, and the whole lot come rattling down. It is not an intellectual amusement—that is the beauty of it— but it is fascinating enough during those early years when the mind still shines in its pristine innocence, and can take its most vivid pleasures in the simplest things.

The book as missile, just mentioned, has been found especially useful in the House of Commons. In the French Chamber of Deputies (from the neighbourhood of which I write these lines), and in the Council Chamber of the Paris Town Hall, they prefer throwing desk-bells, water bottles and tumblers. We, if I remember aright, prefer books. Every

nation has its own political customs, and there is
nothing more foolish (so I am assured) than creating
them artificially. They must be allowed to *grow*.
I have been told that over and over again, so it must
be true; and, after all, the proof is ready to hand.
We have, in this country, no written Constitution,
and it is admitted by everyone in this country that
this country is the happiest, the strongest, the best,
the finest, the noblest in the world. And, by the way,
the modern despotisms have no written constitution
either that I know of—but that is another story.

The book as missile easily surpasses in neatness
the other forms of political artillery, such as the chair,
which has lately appeared in public meetings whirl-
ing through the air like a sort of chain-shot. The
chair, as missile, ought to be forbidden. It is a
barbarous weapon.

Then there is the book as furniture. It has been
too much written about, but one ought to note it in
passing, because to treat books as furniture is at any
rate a better use for them than reading them; moreover it concerns the book as a material object. It
deals with the outside of books which, ninety-nine
times out of a hundred, is better than the inside. I
know not how it is but the covers of books still
remain in tolerably good taste. Architecture has gone,
music has gone, painting and sculpture have gone,
but book-binding remains. The book-binders have
kept their tradition, and their colours are not only
quiet, but blend. It is odd that it should be so. There
is no design about it. The harmonies of bound books

are like the flowers of the field. Go into any library built up by a man who gets his books bound, and see what a fine effect the variegated hues create! So true is this that not a few millionaires have wisely bought up old books (for old bindings, like old everything else, are the best—especially old people), have cut out their insides, leaving only the top and the sides of the pages, and then set them up in a row to furnish their walls. I have seen some very pretty examples of this in the new world, especially striking when the work so gutted was of the seventeenth century, ornamented with heraldic signs. In the same way books are used (having had the insides cut out—mummified books as one might call them, or embalmed books) as work-baskets, but more generally to hold cigarettes. This last is indeed a very noble purpose to which to put a book, especially a book of any antiquity and lineage. It was only the other day that I came upon a first edition of Spinoza's Philosophy, in a fine old Dutch binding, excellently gutted and filled with Turkish or Egyptian smokes—I forget which. A first edition of Dryden's Virgil, especially if it be the large illustrated edition, comes in particularly handy as a work-basket, better than for cigarettes, but any useful service to which a book can be put in this fashion is to be commended.

Books are not much use for weighing things; it is one of their few disadvantages; they are not sufficiently subdivisible. If you are sending something by parcel post and you are too lazy to go to the kitchen, there is a temptation, when you have exhausted the metal weights on your writing table, to pile up a book or two on the scales and make a rough guess at the number of stamps you will need. It is a temptation to be resisted, because the unit is too large and you tend to pay too much for your parcel. Coins are much better if you are one of those wise people who carry great quantities of money about with you in your pockets and so avoid the bother of change, and especially the curse of that redundant disk, the half-penny.

But, while books are of very little use for weighing things, they are excellent as paper weights and especially for keeping down the corners of maps. I know not why it is that when people spread out a map in order to find out who is going to win a war, or to decide on which motor road a painful death shall await them, they nearly always forget that maps are, of their nature, things that curl up. The same is true of kittens and hedgehogs. Men (not women, for women do not use maps) will spread a map out awkwardly with both hands, let go of one edge and see it roll up before their very eyes; then they spread it out again and have all their trouble renewed. Indeed, many map-makers, knowing this trick in maps, cut them up and paste them by sections on linen, but it is a defective way of using maps to have them mounted thus, for you cannot measure distances accurately upon such. With books to hold down the corners the whole thing is solved, and it is the glory of our age that there are always books lying about for this or any other useful purpose over and above the deleterious self-hypnotism called reading.

Some prophets say that books will die, and what may be said of prophets in general we shall see when we come to prophets, if, indeed, we ever come to them in these musings. Meanwhile prophecy is going about confidently, made by the sort of men who prophesy as a trade—they were never more numerous than they are today. The book (they tell us) will die very soon. It will be replaced by a talking machine or whatnot.

Indeed, a friend of mine told me only the other day that one such contraption already existed in the shape of a great cone for which a gramophone record had been taken. You wound it up, you turned it on, and, at any pace that suited you, it whirred or squeaked dull fiction or atheism, or whatever you were in the mood for. Other people say that the book will die, not through the competition of the gramophone record, but through the laying on of hired fiction. You will subscribe to an agency, just as you now subscribe to a library, you will turn a pointer on a dial and a hole in the wall will spout at you the works of Shakespeare or Imperial Problems or Popular Science—what you will. In this way books will be superseded and will die.

It may be so. I have my doubts, for I heard the same thing said about horses when the internal combustion engine appeared, yet horses survive and flourish. So it may be with books. But if books go out, what a revolution! As it is, most books now-a-days

die very quickly, and, as with men, the most deserving die first. One of the best books of the world
(I ought to know, because I wrote it anonymously)
only sold thirty-five copies beyond those which I
bought myself, and then it went the way of all books.
I do not give its name, for to do that would savour
of pride.

Yes, books die rapidly now-a-days. They die in
heaps—but they do not all die. When *all* books are
dead, when no more books are produced, that will
be a revolution indeed! It will be like living in a
world where everything is newspaper and nothing
but newspaper. We have not got to that yet, but
perhaps we are approaching it, for it is a general
rule today that things get worse. But will it be worse
to do without books altogether? I am not so sure.

About Prophecy

I HAVE done a good deal of prophesying in my life most of it wonderfully true and some of it exact. I only ventured once on a precise date and there I was out by miles, but I have made decisions of less precision (this does not rhyme though you think it does) and have been proud of the result. For instance when Bulgaria joined the wrong side in the Great War I boldly prophesied that the first front to break would be the Bulgarian front and that the Allies would pour through. And so they did. I made the prophecy years before it came off and it was rather risky. Also on July 18th, 1918 after the news had come through that Mangin had done the trick on the West side of the Marne pocket I sent a telegram to the newspaper I was writing for in those days saying that the war was won, but they would not publish the telegram because they were afraid. I also prophesied four years ago that the King and Queen of England would pay a visit to the United States, and soon —and so on, plenty of prophecies and most of them bull's eyes but not a penny piece out of any of them. On the other hand I notice with pleasure that other people's prophecies do not come off. I have good cause to know this as I often lay bets against such things and though I win I never get paid. Hitler has recently prophesied, according to reports, saying that he would walk into Warsaw with the greatest ease and that right speedily, but he does not know any

147

more than I do. The great Nüremberg prophecy has come off all right but what I have not been able to track down is the chapter and verse for it. I first saw it in print in the middle of the Great War and I wish I had taken down a copy. It was a number of alternate hexameters and pentameters giving the fate of the Hohenzollern from Albert the Bear onwards, if I remember right. It ended up by saying that the last but two would raise the House to the pinnacle of its fame and power (that was William I, King of Prussia and Emperor of Germany), and that the last but one would have a short and unhappy reign, (that was Frederick of whom it was only too true) and that the last of all, the surviving Emperor Wilhelm or exile of Doorn would be the end of the line. It then added that the ruin of the House would be due to the Jews who would pay for the act of death.

There was another prophecy going around at the time of the Great War saying that the first big victory announcing the end would be won by a nation that had no S in its name—that was not very illuminating, but a better prophecy was that of the Brigadier-General of the Western Front who prophesied that the war would end on the 11th day of the 11th month of the year in which he spoke—1918. That was impressive, but there was a crab about it, he did not publish his prophecy until after the Armistice; when he did he said he had got it out of the Bible, but by that time it was easy going, all clear and the green light. If he had printed it the August before it would have been more impressive. Just after the Germans broke through at St. Quentin it would have been more impressive.

I know a man who heard from a soothsayer to whom he paid a shilling that he would make a great marriage with a very wealthy woman, that he would not care for her nor she for him, and that she would have no effect upon his life, that he would become immensely famous and live in a gigantic house.

Now the man still lives and if all these things are to come off he or fate or somebody must hurry up for at latest reports he is dogged poor, crushed and loaded with debt, lives in a hovel, married for inclination and never had a penny to bless himself with. I do not blame the soothsayer (who by the way was a she not a he, and who practised it at a sort of tent in an Earl's Court Exhibition. Everyone who has to earn a living may be excused a little extravagance in speech), nor do I blame the man for giving the sooth-sayer a shilling, it is a very small sum and he had the fun of looking forward to a pleasant future. Nor do I blame the exhibition for having soothsayers in it, I only wish there were more of them.

As for Old Moore I used to read him every year of my life from the age of about fifteen onwards. I hope he is still going strong for old sake's sake, but I gave him up years ago when he said that nothing remarkable would happen in, but here I stop, for the Lawyers are, many of them, now unemployed and longing for the chance of a libel action. I will not gratify them.

On Fountains

I KNOW not why fountains should have gone out of
fashion. Perhaps because they are beautiful. They
were the life of the great gardens from the Renaissance onwards. They were the glory of the seventeenth century. They had about them all that best
nourishes the mind of man, the right sound, cool-
ness in heat, pleasant and natural motion, innocent
vitality. They were symbolic, too, full of reserva-
tion and of continuity, and they had about them just
enough surprise, just enough artifice, to bear witness
to the creative power of man. They were more than
ornaments—far more—they were companions; and
their movements corresponded to the movements of
the air, majestic in calm, lively in a strong breeze.
Once a man had got used to fountains playing near
his house, he could no more do without them than
without any other consonant companion.

It has been said that of all friends, humanity will
grow most attached to friends inanimate. That is
not quite true. There are exceptions. One can even
get strongly attached to one or two human beings,
and attachment to dogs is notorious. But there is
this about inanimate companionship: that it never
betrays or quarrels. We put much of ourselves into
it and it amply repays the loan. Now of such inanimate companions I would, after great landscape, put
fountains first. For, while they are inanimate, yet
have they such a vivacity about them and such an

unending, strong but easy effort, that they continually suggest life.

Also the unity of fountains answers to the unity of human experience. For the fountain, like the human life, is one thing. We give it one name. We are nourished by its continuation. It is even more one thing than a human life because it is not of its nature doomed to fail, but continues unendingly. Yet, like a human life, it is not, save at one moment, itself, but a succession; and its oneness, if not an illusion, is at any rate something spiritual, for you could make no material definition of it.

There is this also about fountains. That they witness to the spontaneous in mankind. For what model ever had our fathers to suggest such things? The fountain would seem to be the only human ornament which is wholly made by man. I think some good Power taught him how to make the first fountain, and there is this extra good about fountains, that they are not a development; they arrived full grown. On this account, also, the fountain is almost the only realised figment of man's fancy which has not been murdered by excess. I know not what your experience may be, but mine is that no man ever boasted of the *height* of his fountain. No man ever thought his fountain better than his neighbour's, because the water of it was thrown higher into the air. The one test has always been beauty and sufficiency. That is not true of any other thing that man makes, I am afraid, least of all is it true of towers, which are a sort of parallel to fountains, doing the things fountains do, rising up into space and aiming at the sky. An exaggeration of towers has tempted men from the beginning. Hence Babel; and Beckford, being too rich, could think of nothing better than to make the very tallest tower imaginable—and it fell down. But fountains have always kept due measure.

Fountains are not immaterial, but they are the nearest simulacrum of spiritual things. They cannot grow old. There is no decay about them. What a man knew them to be in his youth, that he finds them still in his old age, and were the great King to return to Versailles, in *these* he would not be disappointed.

I had almost written that fountains are not subject to heresy or to mis-use, but this again is not quite true, for the orthodox fountain, which is by right a jet, dependent for its spring and vigour upon a concealed head of water, higher than itself, may be simulated by a very unorthodox contraption: I mean a fountain working by machine. There are fountains thus monstrously made which only leap into the air because the source from which they are drawn is subject to compression of the air above it.

Indeed I knew a man once who made for his garden a fountain which thus used the same water over and over again. I do not believe it was ever accepted by real fountains as one of their company. I doubt its admission to the Fountain Club. Such base pseudo-fountains are the product of modern town governments, water laid on and doled out through a meter. But a true fountain is free, not servile, and proper to the gardens of freemen at the least, and, at the greatest, to the gardens of great nobles, Popes and moneylenders.

There are even, alas! some false fountains which cover something baser yet and are pumped up by engines; yes, some of them, by that invention of the devil the internal combustion engine itself. These fountains, which can hardly be called fountains at all, bear upon them the mark of the beast in the shape of noise. The unnatural, repeated, unorganic hammer of the piston, not wholly concealed, ruins all.

That is abominable, for if there is one thing about a fountain more divine than another, it is the way in which the sound of it is a benediction, married to nature all around. One shall come upon a fountain which some wise man designed in the days when Europe was Europe; a fountain rising from a marble round, situated in an open glade, overshadowed by great trees. Come on such a fountain and you have come upon something which is at once part of the nature about you and more than that nature, something which inspires and makes alive in a special way all the leaves and branches of the place, all the air.

The fountain has relatives in its family, humbler than itself and discoverable without the aid of man —notably the cascade. But there is nothing like itself, except itself (as Swift said of the elephant); there is no other work of man which is so simple and so single, so satisfying, so complete, so full and so successful a challenge to the shadow of mortality and to the burden of change. For though the fountain is ever in movement, it is ever one in strength and character: young when we were young and still young when we are grown old. That is why there always seems to be something of murder about the dereliction of a fountain, the letting of it go dry; and when one comes upon a rusted fountain, dead (as in the unhappy example of Chalons and I know not how many other tragic relics of a better time), one always laments a sordid death.

Go you, therefore, and make fountains about your gardens. I say it with the less hesitation because I shall not have to pay for them. But after all they are not costly things, and if you can afford to have a garden at all you can surely afford to have a fountain which shall baptize it continually and give it perennial grace.

So much for fountains.

On Town Walls

A BETTER term is "city walls"; that is the traditional phrase; but I would not use it here for fear of its getting mixed up with the wall of the City of London, of which I am not writing here in any detail.

One of the products of the long peace in England (never seriously interrupted save during a few years after Charles I's reign—between the Raising of the Standard and Naseby) is that we have no walled towns —or as near as makes no difference. The western continent has plenty of them. There is a crowd of names. There is Avila, there is Leon, there is Avignon, of which I was writing the other day. There is Ronda; there is the very fine example close at hand of St. Malo, in Brittany. There are, perhaps, hundreds of European examples—scores of them still perfect —but within this island the walled town no longer appears to the eye. Chester is the closest thing to it, I suppose. Even in Chester the walls do not make part of the landscape; they stand, for a great length of them, in the midst of buildings.

Yet before the Civil Wars, and even for a good time after, indeed, you may say, up to the time when the effects of the industrial revolution first began to be felt in the sudden growth of the population, especially in industrial and commercial places, the walled town was the one characteristic thing of any English prospect so far as building and human work were concerned. Men travelled mainly on horseback; later, for a while, largely by coach. The Englishman thus moving about England on his lawful occasions would carry home with him memories of one walled town after another, each defined by its walls as by a frame. The walls were the first thing he saw as he approached any city from afar, for its spires and towers it would have in common with any village or other small human group, but the *walls* were the mark of the important town.

* * *

All that has gone. The English landscape is now so innocent of the walled town that Englishmen no longer remember it. There are venerable fragments here and there. Notable is the fragment on the south side of Canterbury where, if I remember aright, something of the moat also remains, and very remarkable is the last fragment of the Oxford wall standing in the midst of New College. London has slight remains which do not commonly meet the eye, and one could make a list of perhaps twenty or thirty exceptions of this kind, but the walled town has gone. Unlike the great mass of our antiquities, it has not survived its function.

No other country has preserved the fossils, or shells, of a past time as England has. That preservation is due in part to the almost uninterrupted peace of over 400 years (especially the absence of civil revolution and partisan fighting), partly to the great increase of wealth which has provided funds for the antiquaries; partly to the excellence of the administration.

Here I am tempted to a digression. Administration in England has been so continuously excellent that this confusion between government and administration flatters the national mind. We call any foreign country that is well administered "well governed"; yet the idea of government is distinct indeed from the idea of administration. For government is the ordering of men's minds. It is a spiritual force. Administration is but the ordering of their routine. It is no more than a mechanical thing.

So much for that. Anyhow, we have for various reasons accumulated a greater wealth by far in the material evidence of the past than has any other European country. That accumulation has been neither spoilt by neglect nor destroyed in civil or invading war.

*   *   *

Well, the thing which marked out all our countryside, the walled town, a thing everywhere and especially in the closest neighbouring part of the continent still common, has disappeared from among us.

When I hear the word "Chichester", a town which I should know best in Europe, for it was the market town and local capital of my youth, I forget that it ever had a circuit of walls and that their remains can still be traced among the houses; yet anyone thinking of Sussex up to quite modern times remembered Chichester as a walled town. People coming in by the sea plain from the west, or from the east, or across the downs from the north, were aware of the walls long before they noted anything else, except, beyond them, the spire of the Cathedral. The people of Chichester rebuilt their spire, much as it had been, for Sussex is the most conservative of the English counties. But, for all its attachment to ancient things, Sussex did not keep Chichester as a walled town: a pity, I think. It is when we have lost things that we know their meaning—and then it is too late.

Look how the business of mankind, since first men were taught by Gods and Heroes to live in cities, has magnified such walls! On a city wall Helen walked and Andromache fell down in darkness at the sight of Hector dead. Against the walls of Rome her chief enemy cast his spear as a symbol, but in vain. It was a threat to the walls of Athens that was felt to be a threat to the very soul the city. The walls of Paris withstood the barbarians of the northern sea, and it was when the Lombard cities rebuilt their walls that they proved their victory in the long struggle against the invader from across the mountains. When Charlemagne would mark his triumphant ride beyond the Pyrenees by throwing down the walls of Pamplona; and Jericho, which never did much, can at least boast that its walls showed in a startling fashion their dislike of rough music. The greatest of the capitals, Babylon, Pekin, gloried in the magnitude of their walls. Travellers have told me that these last, the Chinese example, are still the most arresting piece of building in the world.

Yes, all history and all literature are full of the walled town; and yet it is so unfamiliar to us in England to-day that our historians never visualise it. Our writers of historical fiction—a department in which, like the French, we excel—are rather better at remembering the habitations of their fathers; yet even they commonly leave out that major physical condition and boundary, the town wall. With the passing of it there has passed the idea of an exact city limit, of a sharp division between the townsman and the countryman. There has passed also with it one of the most sacred of human things—the Guarded Gate.

On Advertisement

FISHES DO not know that they live in water. They think they live in the world at large, and very glad they are to be in so comfortable an air. When you take them out of the water into the real air they object, they protest, they kick, they gasp and they die. This is by way of telling you (if you did not know it already) that men do not grasp the characteristics of the place and time in which they live. That place and time have become part of their nature. They have long ceased to imagine anything other. And when you tell them that their environments are only those of the place and time in which they live, they either protest or tell you it is unimportant.

Now the characteristic of the place and time in which we live, here and today, is advertisement. It is by the universal presence of advertisement that our lives differ from those of our fathers. It is by the obsession of advertisement that our minds are moved in a manner peculiar to our generation, unknown to earlier generations and (please God!) to be equally strange to future generations. Not only things for sale, advertised by those who desire us to buy them, but false characters, false fame, false ill-repute, are drummed into us morning, noon and night. Repetition has taken the place of emphasis and of reasoning. In that which men most eagerly pursue—I mean wealth—advertisement conditions everything.

Next to wealth, perhaps, what men desire is being

talked about. It is a strange thing to want, but a great part of mankind do want it, especially in youth. Now to be talked about today you must be advertised. Indeed, men are not talked about at all nowadays unless they are advertised. Though the dead should rise, they would need advertisement. And the converse is true. If you would persuade men that the dead had risen having no other proof whatsoever of something so extraordinary, sufficient repetition of the falsehood would do the work.

Through advertisement all values are today sent awry. Each of us meets among a numerous acquaintance some few men who powerfully affect his mind, having more knowledge or more wisdom or more intensity than the rest. If they have more knowledge or more wisdom they are of high value to their fellows. If they, added to knowledge or to wisdom, have a desire to propagate such truths as they have discovered, they are of the highest value to their fellows. Yet none will know of them; while all will know too thoroughly the *names* at least of the advertised.

There is a consequence following on so strange and, let us hope, so ephemeral a state of affairs. It is this: that those who control the gates of advertisement are the masters of commerce and of opinion. Those who have in their possession the machinery (particularly through the press) of repeating that this or that should be bought, that this or that is good, that this or that is wonderful, that this or that is true, hold and will hold the power to proclaim or to impose silence. For some time past these "masters of the gate" (and in our urban modern way of living they are but a handful) were principally content with levying a toll, saying to the advertisers "you shall not pass through my gate until you have paid so much each." The vast revenues they thus captured were at first sufficient for them. But there came upon them gradually, what more intelligent men would have discovered earlier in the business, the discovery that they could act positively as well as negatively. They could not only levy a toll but command. They could refuse or obstruct or encourage the passage through the gate. This gave them power, which, like fame and money, is very much desired by men; and so the masters of advertisement came not only to great fortunes but also to ruling.

Providence has so happily disposed the world that men desiring money and (in a less degree) men desiring fame, and (in a still less degree) men desiring power, are commonly stupid in proportion to the strength of such desires in them. Were it not so the harm done by the controllers of advertisement would be infinite. As it is, through their stupidity the harm is limited. But it is growing, as day by day the men upon whom advertisement depends discover and enlarge their opportunities. Their effect is as good an example as one could get of the universal truth, that evil comes from the substitution of the means for the end.

Are there limits to this evil? It is growing, manifestly. It is worse now by far than it was even a quarter of a century ago. It is far worse than it was fifty years ago. Yet anyone who will look at the thing dispassionately, without allowing his disgust for the vileness of it to deflect his judgment, must admit that the disease does tend to a maximum and therefore to a limit; and, what is more, in that tendency to a maximum and to a limit we shall find the ultimate remedy for this disease. It will not be a remedy (alas!) of our own choosing. It will be a remedy imposed, as perhaps are most remedies to epidemics, by the nature of things.

Advertisement tends to a maximum and therefore to a limit in many ways. First of all it depends on repetition, and yet fatigues by that very repetition. It does not weary the crowd as soon as it wearies the more cultivated or the more contemplative, but at last it wearies even the crowd.

Then there is the tendency to a maximum, and therefore to a limit through the exaggeration of competition, and through the decay of competition through merger. In commercial affairs this is evident. The fierce battle of advertisements between two rival sellers dies down because they are rivals no longer but have combined to bleed the public. There are whole departments of goods and services in which this slackening of advertisement through merger is already manifest. It is no doubt a bad remedy for a bad thing, but it *is* a remedy. It would seem that the only obstacle to such tendencies is that general merger of all control in one despotic centre, which is just now so fashionable a panacea for the misfortunes of human society. In the despotism, where all competition is under control, any branch of it may be killed at a moment's notice. But the despotisms themselves are founded upon advertisement—and advertisement carried to monstrous, inhuman lengths. Some name, some policy, some "slogan" (to use the jargon of advertisers) is shouted till men are deafened with it. Indeed, the modern despotisms would seem to be the very deification of advertisement. Yet under them particular advertisement dies, and that is the end of advertisement by powerful competing individuals. Satiety will do its work at last in this major case also. It looks as though here, as in much else, we shall not return to sanity and reasonable right living until there has been catastrophe. An unhappy conclusion! But it is the conclusion to which one road after another leads as we follow the misfortunes of our time.

When advertisement in every form has lost its power through excess, there will at last return, slowly and imperceptibly in a society grown barbaric and therefore simple, the proper process of fame, of commerce and the rest of it: the attainment of what men desire, not through publicity and its repetition, but rather, as it was in better times, publicity and reputation coming as a natural fruit of living action. Men may then once more be famous for what they have done. Their characters may be admired or detested through the good or the evil of their deeds and we shall be free once more to judge things as they are.

On Hats

HIGH UP in the class of foolish and false common-
places is the commonplace that clothes do not matter.
On the contrary, it is clothing that makes the man.
The Americans have a memorable saying, packed
with stuff, like so many of their lapidary phrases, and
true as true. It runs: "You go on your clothes." Walk
down the street and recall to yourself, after a few
hundred yards, how you have judged the many unknown who have passed you. Why did you think
this one a man of wealth, that one a man of leisure,
that one a poorish man, that one a destitute, wretched
man, that other one a secure, well-established man?
You will find in every case it was what the man wore
which counted for your judgment, and, what is more,
counted for the whole of it. The man who cannot
help being ill-dressed is to be pitied, like any other
defective. The man who tells you that he is indifferent to his dress is either a boaster or a fool.

Now of all the things that men wear, by far the
most important is the Hat. I use the word "Hat" to
mean head-covering of any sort, and I beg you to
mark how, more than any other feature whatever,
the hat, the headgear, differentiates mankind. In
nothing has man been more inventive, in nothing
more various, in nothing symbolic more effective.
You have but to make a list of hats to see how true
that is, beginning with the Tiara and continuing
through the Cardinal's hat and the Mitre and the

Biretta and the Mortar-board and the Square Cap
of the theologians (in the days when there were
theologians) and the Helmet and the Képi and the
Shako and the Vizored Helm and the Conical hat
of steel which recalls the first Crusade, and on till
you get to the Top Hat, now still surviving, though
struggling for life. Every one of them suggests at
once a profession or a caste or a trade or a nationality
or an epoch. This is not true of boots; it is not true
of the general covering of the body. It *is* true of hats.

When we describe in men something much greater
or much less than man, we say it is suitable, not for
human-beings, but for "a beast or for a god". That
is how Aristotle talks of loneliness, for he says that
in order to live without society one must be a beast
or a god. Well, I would have you know that the two
kinds of living things that wear no hats are beasts
and gods.

When we put a hat on a beast we shame the poor
thing. I never knew a cat yet, nor a dog, that did not
worry to get rid of a hat when it found itself deco-
rated with the same. And as for gods, though I have
not come across any since I was fifteen, I have seen
a great number of their portraits, both as busts and
full length, all over the world and I have noted that
they hardly ever have hats. Neither have the demi-
gods or heroes.

There are exceptions of course, because there are
exceptions to everything. Ares wears a casque and
feathers forbye, and Athene wears one sometimes of
a most becoming sort, right on the back of her head,

as the gayer youths of the 'nineties wore their billy-cocks. And Mercury wears a little hat with winglets on it, and now and then Apollo wears a soft felt Phrygian cap, and Mithras always wears one. But, taking the gods and goddesses by and large, they disdain hats and go hatless—an aureole is the most they will tolerate. So was it also with the great mortals of antiquity. They appear in marble, striking an attitude, but always concerned with their dignity and therefore spurning the use of hats. Whoever saw Cicero or Demosthenes or Julius Caesar in a hat? Hats show also a distinction between Orientals and ourselves. The Orientals had a weakness for hats, and some of our most pompous adornments of this kind come from the East, to the disgust of the Roman Tories.

Hats also connote qualities, as well as classes and nations. For instance, your barbarian was never so happy as when he had a sort of hairy beast's head on top of his own, preferably with horns attached to it. If I may trust the pictures (which I do not), those unsympathetic people the Pagan Danes or Norsemen of old (pirates, robbers and murderers at large), affected a headgear of this kind; copied from oxen.

To return to the Americans, I recall another expressive phrase of theirs, when they would denounce pride. They say of the proud man that "he wears a high hat". I very well remember a young man, infected with a Balliol accent, being warned by his American friends and relatives to conceal it as well as he could when he went shopping, whether on the

Atlantic or the Pacific coast. "If you talk like that," he was told, "they will think you are high-hatting them." And since he learnt that lesson, he has carefully avoided such an accent, or even the common speech of the Englishman, *Locutio vulgaris,* whenever he finds himself in the States.

But why wander beyond the Atlantic to the distant, almost fabulous, land of the Hesperides? Have we no hats at home over and above those here so casually catalogued?

Why yes! And in battalions, not in single spies. For instance, as an example of the "effective symbol", what about the policeman's hat—the hat of the English (I beg your pardon, I mean the British) policeman? There is nothing like it on earth save the hat (or is it called the helmet?) of the Spanish policeman in time of peace. Not, indeed, of the Civil Guard who are, or rather who were before the war in Spain, a sort of super policemen, but of the town or common or garden policemen. This in Spain had followed the English model and very odd and out of place it looked—especially in Saragossa, where I first marvelled at it in the good years that never will return.

The policeman's hat or helmet was designed for use rather than for beauty, and certainly not as an effective symbol. Yet that is what it has become. It was thought out most thoroughly: a protection against blows from above and an addition to the stature of the wearer: a muniment—and yet quite light. I know from friends who have put on these

couvrechefs, after playfully abstracting them from
their owners on Boat Race night, that they in no
way burden the head and leave the great brain which
they protect free to plan all good for the Commonwealth which that brain also protects. "For order,"
says Sir Charles Lumbrough, O.B.E., "is the first
requisite in a Commonwealth." He is wrong there.
The first requisite is virtue, and especially the virtue
of justice—but let that go; it would lead us far.

Since things are dying all around us at such a rate
as never was before, I wonder whether hats will not
also die? Many say they are not necessary, but mere
ornaments, wherefore the Sphinx, addressing a traveller from Gaul who had no Greek, put her riddle
thus:—

"Je suis un ornement qu'on porte sur la tête.
Je m'appelle chapeau; devine grosse bête."

But I contest that view. A hat is necessary against
the sun. It is even necessary against cold (except,
for some reason I do not understand, in the city of
London, where hats are not worn). Nevertheless, useful though it is, as well as decorative, the hat may well
disappear. I, for one, should regret it, as I regret
the passing of any custom or of any tradition, for
these are the furniture of human life.

On Statistics

PROPERLY SPEAKING, what I am now about to write should not appear as an essay at all. It is rather an excerpt from a great work now in process of writing, and demanding years and years of labour, called "Lying". This work is designed in twenty-four volumes, but it may well run to thirty before it is completed. But as there is a difficulty in getting a publisher, you shall have a foretaste of it. Perhaps it will advertise the thing and make some publisher relent. Publishers have a way of telling the truth in this matter as in all others. They say to the writing man (poor beast!): "Your subject is fascinating and your work will have the greatest effect. You will write it as no one else could have written it. But as things are now, the chances of sale would hardly warrant the expense of production." There is a healthy air of reality about that!

It has long been recognized by public men of all kinds (whether the talkers or the scribblers or the mere Born-So), that statistics come under the head of Lying, and that no lie is so false or inconclusive as that which is based on statistics. The reason is simple. As truth depends upon proportion, so falsehood has, for its best method, suggestion by wrong proportion. When you are dealing with mere figures you can wangle any proportion you like. You have only to leave out the words which would give the heart of the matter, and your false effect is produced automatically. For instance: look at this account of London just after the death of a great Whig.

"What the effect on London was can best be shown by statistics. We know from these that, for over five hours, the whole life of the great capital came to a standstill. A small minority still engaged in necessary labours, but the general activities of men ceased, as though in a City of the Dead. The familiar rumble of traffic in the streets was hushed. The windows, even of the West End, were darkened. The cries of the newsboys were suspended. So deep was the silence that the footstep of the passer-by re-echoed, as might those of a chance traveller venturing into the ruins of a deserted capital."

That is the way dear old Macaulay would have put it, and very impressive the manner is, especially with a footnote like this: "Of the total population, already numbering in those days over a million, it was estimated by a careful contemporary (whose investigation has been since supported by more modern research) that nineteen-twentieths lay, for these five hours, speechless and almost without motion—See Gamble and Stodge, *The Great Silence,* and the return presented to the House of Commons, of which a copy lies before me as I write."

That is how it is done, and all by not telling you that the hours in question were those of a December night, from one to six in the morning.

Before the curse of statistics fell upon mankind we lived a happy, innocent life, full of merriment and go, and informed by fairly good judgment. We knew

when the weather was cold and when it was dry; we
knew what public opinion was; we knew what was
good for us and what was bad for us, and all the rest.
That state of affairs lasted for centuries. It was too
good to last. The statistician was let loose. He came
in the train of Discovery and the rest. He was part
of Progress. He took up his authority in a world
which could only count and was ceasing to think or
to feel. He appealed to those who had learnt to read
figures and to add up and to multiply and to spell,
but who had learnt nothing else, who were even
rapidly unlearning all things worth knowing. Until
the coming of this enemy to the human mind we
rejoiced in the spring weather, and we said: "What
a delightful day!" We did not know that the rainfall
was .00215 above the average. We were indignant to
hear of a brutal murder. We did not know that brutal
murderers wax and wane with the waxing and waning
of sun-spots—flourishing when these are extensive,
halting when these are less. We knew that a good
bottle of wine was a good bottle of wine, and a bottle
of methylated something quite other. Now we learn
from statistics that each has such and such an amount
—"percentage" they call it—of a whimsy dubbed
"Alcohol", and that therefore wine and methylated
are the same. We knew an Englishman when we saw
him. We did not know that the facial angle, the
cephalic index, let alone the lachrymary gland, could
prove by figures that Englishmen were not Englishmen at all, but something other. We knew that we
had to die, but we did not know that the average

expectation of life in anyone who had reached the age of five years and forty-two days was—whatever it is. Our childhood was the less troubled. We knew that flying into a passion was undignified, futile and (for the apoplectic) dangerous. But no one strapped little gadgets round our arms and talked mumbo-jumbo about blood pressure, and proved us ready for heaven. We knew when we were oppressed by taxation, we knew when the oppression had become intolerable, and having sound general instincts in the matter, we could correct the evil; but once it was proved to us that of the total national income only half or whatever it is, was really subject to taxation, we persuaded ourselves it was all right—yes, even when we had to give up the car.

Statistics are the triumph of the quantitative method, and the quantitative method is the victory of sterility and death. The sane, unspoilt mind comes at truth by integration: you see a tree and say: "That is an elm." The diseased statistical mind counts the leaves and measures the shapes thereof, working by differentials.

Nowhere has your statistical falsehood done more harm than in the department of letters. In every field of that supreme activity it has spread pestilence and blight. Did you believe that some inspired recital struck to the very heart of things and revealed a divine world? You were disabused by a German, or rather a horde of Germans, who came waddling along with analyses of text, counting, most curiously, how many times *kurios* appeared, and finding contrast be-

tween the repetitions of *alla gar* and *men . . . de*.
Homer ceased to be Homer, and, what is more,
"statistics showed" that he had hardly any vocabu-
lary. Troy shrank to be a little quadrangle, the sides
of which were paced out. The Persian host became
a few battalions and Marathon a skirmish.

Is there a remedy to this plague? Yes, there are
two remedies mercifully provided. The first remedy
is the extinction of statistics by their own excess.
A new batch of them perpetually wipes out the last
batch. The double analysis kills the single analysis,
and the treble kills the double, until at last a sufficiency of statistics comes very near to common sense.

But the second remedy is much the best. When
our mechanical civilization, if civilization it can still
be called, shall die the sudden death which it is so
industriously preparing, statistics will die with it;—
and so shall we.

The Wisdom of the White Knight

THE WHITE KNIGHT in *Alice in Wonderland* made distinctions which in my youth I thought to be folly, juggling with words and all the tiresome business of what used to be called "nonsense humour". But in the course of years experience showed me that there was something in it, and now after something like a lifetime (I think I first read *Alice in Wonderland* somewhere about 1888), I find in that passage of the White Knight's conversation a deep well of wisdom.

Alice and the White Knight were discussing a song. Alice (if I remember rightly), when she was told the name of the song says: "Oh, that is what the song is called, is it?" The White Knight answers: "Not at all; that is not what the song is called, that is the name of the song." Then he tells her what the song is called, which is something very different from the name; and when she says, "Oh, that is what the song is, is it?" he again takes her up: "No, that is not what the song is, that is what the song is called; the song is so and so." Doubtless I have not got the words right, nor the replies in their right order. Nor does that matter in the least. The White Knight's wisdom lies in the distinction he makes between three things, which a lax mind identifies but which a keen mind differentiates.

Most of the harm done by words comes from the folly of using words indeterminately. And for some reason on which I am not clear—perhaps fatigue—

our modern urban civilisation in use of English is getting to use more and more words without outlines or edges, without precision.

Take for example the word "majority". You could turn that word round in the light (if you will take it close to the window) and look at one facet after another, and each you will find to bring you a different aspect of it. To put the matter without metaphor and accurately, the words "a majority" if they are left undefined can mean almost anything. The appeal to a majority comes of course from political habit. We are always reading of majorities cast thus or thus, and always being told that they are overwhelming or decisive, or what not. But a majority means nothing until you are clear upon quite a number of things about it. For instance, is it a majority upon a subject which the people consulted know enough about for a decision to represent a real conviction, or even a real inclination? Of whom is it a majority? Of all the men and boys over 18 or 21 or 24, of all the men and boys over 18 and all the women and girls over 18 as well? Is it a spontaneous majority? Is it an enthusiastic majority, or a reluctant majority, or even an indifferent majority?

100 people vote on whether tea shall be forbidden by law or not (I will not say alcohol because that would lead one into another labyrinth of definition and into any amount of back chat as well: I say tea because it is an example which can be discussed without passion). 100 people, I say, are asked to vote on the question whether tea should be forbidden by

law. I will suppose that there has been a good deal of propaganda, as it is called, by the Anti-Tea Party for some time past, emphasising the horrors of tea, giving stories of people who have gone mad through drinking too much tea, printing as a pamphlet the vivid and terrifying story of Le Fanu called "Green Tea". Then there might be a cross-section of propaganda. The Anti-Tea people describe perhaps bad cases of oppression on tea plantations, and so forth. Now one could see how an Anti-Tea Party could be formed, although to begin with everybody either liked tea or was indifferent to it. Well, you take the vote by men only. After propaganda has done its work, you take it in a district where there is a mixed English and foreign population and you get not quite two-thirds of the registered voters giving their verdict. There are 1000 registered voters—all of them over 18. 600 vote. Of these 600, 310 vote for the suppression of tea; 290 vote for being allowed to go on drinking tea as they have been drinking it all their lives, can't get on without it; it is agony to them to be deprived of their cup of tea. The 310 are a majority, although nearly all of them care next to nothing about the business and most of them have been dragooned into voting. What does such a "majority right" mean? Less than one-third of the adult male population, less than one-sixth of the total population have a lukewarm passion to put down their mark for the Anti-Tea ticket—and behold! you may have no tea in the name of democracy.

And what about the word "efficiency"? Efficiency

towards what end? A friend who lives on the Marches of Wales told me the other day that some Government person or another was very eager to enlist his influence against the use of the Welsh language in certain schools. He said that young people who grew up knowing Welsh rather than English were less efficient. My friend answered, "Less efficient in what? Welsh literature?" He happens to be a zealot for Welsh literature, so he felt strongly. The question was quite legitimate. You can have a system in your office or even in your home which is more efficient towards the saving of expense and less efficient towards comfort. You can have a machine which is more efficient towards rapid production and less efficient towards accurate production. The word "efficient" has been used continually since Lord Rosebery launched it for popular consumption perhaps 40 years ago. I have heard it used in 1,000 places and never once with any clear understanding by the speaker of what he meant. Yet in the name of efficiency characters are warped, homes are destroyed, a hideous building takes the place of beauty, and insane haste the place of decent leisure.

But the worst of the whole gang is the word "able". It came from the Universities, largely I think in order to supplant the older and still sillier word "clever", which had come to have a slightly derogatory flavour about it. Able at what? "I found John Smith a very able man." "What, on horseback?" "Oh, no, he couldn't ride." "At woodcarving?" "Certainly not." "At secret poisoning, terse writing, card tricks, ventriloquism, repartee, novel, variegated and original cursing?" "No, none of those things. He was just an able man." "Well, for instance?" "Oh, if you want an instance, he put the finances of the College on their feet again after old Biddleworth had mangled everything up." "I see, Mr Smith was able at keeping accounts and managing money."

Now, how could anybody know Mr Smith's talents, character, value, from that original word "able"? Yet on the repetition of that word 100 reputations have been built.

Landscapes

THERE ARE certain great landscapes which impressed themselves strongly upon the minds of our grandfathers and their forebears before the coming of the industrial revolution and the railway. One of these was the Ebro Valley seen by the traveller who passes the Pyrenees in summer at the Somport on his way to Madrid.

There were not many such, for the main ways of getting into Spain were at either end of the mountain range; either by the pass of Pertuis (of which we have heard so much lately) or by the bridge across the Bidassoa and the town of Irun—of which we heard so much two years ago. People seldom crossed the Pyrenees by the central approach—a high and difficult pass which had no proper road over it between Roman and quite modern times, but remained for centuries a mule track. It was little known in the later centuries of coach travel, yet it was the best introduction to Spain, not only because from that approach one could see and feel what a barrier the Pyrenees were, but also because, as one came down the banks of Aragon, there came a point whence the whole majestic width of the Ebro Valley lay some hundreds of feet below one, and beyond, the solemn massive bulk of the Moncayo mountain standing like a solid cloud, grey, far, permanent and very high.

Another such landscape was the view from a lift in the road of the Lake of Bolsena which broke upon all

men taking the main way to Rome, for centuries—
I mean the way, not along the sea coast but direct
through Etruria, southward. That Lake of Bolsena,
the trees upon the edges of its vast walled circle of
water, filled the imagination of painters for generations. The students who came from the north to the
Roman schools all saw it and remembered it. It was
not often exactly reproduced on canvas, but one
can find, over and over again in a hundred examples,
the memory of it haunting northern painters, particularly those of the seventeenth century.

*　　*　　*

There was a whole lifetime during which these
landscapes which so impressed the traveller by road
were eclipsed by railway travel. The first piercing of
the Alps is nearly contemporary with my own birth.
The first general use of steam for travel into Spain
came later, but, in general, the generation to which
I belong lived, during its useful years, through a time
when the specially fine landscapes were not experienced by the bulk of travellers. Railways (like Lord
Burghley's Scotsmen) "do not climb." It means expense; and to avoid that horrid misfortune they keep
to the level and to the valleys. They will even bur-
row underground rather than enjoy the view from
a pass.

One would have thought that with the coming of
the internal combustion engine the great views would
return—or, at least, some of them. One would have
thought that the main great views, like that one over

the Ebro Valley and that other over Bolsena Lake, would become again part of the furniture of the European mind. It ought to have been so, but, as usual, there has been a crab. One might generalise and say that nothing good ever returns, at least in its completeness. The motor-car goes so fast and (what is psychologically more important) the people who drive it are so eaten up with speed that they hardly see a landscape at all. Only those very wise ones who go slowly (and destroy their machinery by an excess of such leisure) have some idea of what a landscape seen from a road may be. Most modern travellers can remember flashes rather than land-scapes. The vision is hardly apparent when it is already gone. It does not remain and take root. It does not become a companion. It does not remain an enduring part of personality.

The best way of all for approaching landscape— which is on foot—has survived indeed, but not suffi-ciently survived. And the next best way (which is on horseback, or, better still, donkeyback and mule-back) can be still indulged as an eccentricity, but it is not commonly known. I can never be too thankful for having crossed the Apennines upon a mule by a narrow path above the Trebbia Valley. I had the good fortune on that occasion to come upon a glade in the heights wherein were disporting themselves not a few of the younger pagan gods and goddesses. But travel of this kind is very rare.

*   *   *

It is a wise thing while one is still young to seek out great landscape, by pottering about in hill country, having first judged from the map where probably some wide revelation of the earth may be enjoyed. Most of such points of vantage are remote from a road. Nearly all of them have the very great drawback that one must approach them uphill. What a drawback that is few nowadays admit save in their secret hearts. At any rate, it has this countervailing advantage that it keeps the great visions private and personal. One shall come upon such and such a view by accident, following a footpath or crossing open land.

I remember one from the edge of the Jura where there was no road and whence one looked from the height above a precipice right over Switzerland to the Bernese mountains. And I remember another on the shoulder of Plinlymmon looking northward towards Cader Idris, which frowned awfully in an inky black steep against the sky. A man who walks a great deal in youth comes upon a multitude of such things.

I do not know whether it is a misfortune or a boon to the world that those who write, although they are often the same as those who travel, are not the same as those who climb at random over ill-known places. I think I have discovered the reason, though it puzzled me for some years to know what it was; it is that those who have the leisure to explore delights in this fashion are under no necessity to write or to publish their experiences for the benefit of their fellow-men. That also has good attached to it, though writers would be slow to admit it. The good is this: if all men who had wealth and leisure and used them for the discovery of loveliness were to set their visions down in black and white they would vulgarise the beauty of this world. They are doing it quite enough as it is. With which charitable thought, farewell.

About Volcanoes

THE OTHER day I was standing on a hill in Tuscany, overlooking a noble sweep of country to the east which was the heart of the ancient Etruria. It is one of the most interesting countrysides in the world, because it gave its religion and its early Kings to Rome, and also because its origins are so mysterious. No one really knows where the Etruscans came from nor (what is more important) where their religious tradition came from—a tradition in which they seem to be unique, and one which has so strongly and permanently affected, from their time to this, all European civilisation.

On that height, with that prospect before us, a companion who was with me said: "No civilisation without volcanoes." This was a whimsical and partial truth which I had not come across before. This old Tuscan land is a mass of dead volcanoes and their formation continues on to the south.

*   *   *

It is not true to say there is no civilisation without volcanoes. There have been plenty of civilisations without volcanoes. But volcanoes do give a fillip to a culture, and wherever you have volcanoes, dead or alive, you have something distinct from the rest of the world.

So it is here in Tuscany. O dark, creative, veiled, and fathomless Etruria! How can a man write one word upon you without the sense of awe! Surely it is a land of the gods, and here are the tombs of those great Lords and their Ladies that should make Corneto—which is also Tarquinia—as famous a city as any in the world, for it is a bridge between the living and the dead. Here may you see those mighty men and women sculptured in volcanic stone, half rising from their tombs, expectant yet assured. They look on immortality and new things. Their ancient sepultures have been dug into the hill for miles, where the height overlooks a distant shore: frontier between this life and another. For there lies beneath them, an hour's march away, and fully displayed, the broad level of the sea into which the sun sets evening by evening, beckoning to the west.

Here in Tuscany the old volcanoes are, and have been for centuries, silent. Their craters are filled with solemn lakes, some of great size. So are the craters of the dead volcanoes beyond. The lakes of the Alban hills lie in old craters—the famous lake of Nemi, the as famous and more lovely Alban lake, on which I propose to write again.

*   *   *

Someone pursuing this odd theme of the connection between volcanoes and a vivid culture might remark that volcanic soil produces the best of wine. One might suggest that the excellence of wine so grown accounts for the excellence of the verse and prose and for the profundity of the philosophy which hangs about volcanic hills. It would be simpler, less irrational or mystical (and therefore more in keeping with the spirit of our time), to call the connection between volcanoes and deep thinking fortuitous. I am not so sure.

Consider Iceland and consider Sicily. Those two islands are very different. But they have this in common—that each is lively with a volcano and each has left its particular stamp on letters and, therefore, on mankind. The north never did anything so strong (scholars assure me) as the Icelandic verse in the turn between pagan and Christian times; and I hope that most people know the connection between Sicily and Vulcan. Now of Sicily was written that lovely line I quote too often: "The sheep all grazing down together towards the Sicilian sea."

It was written (I think) by Theocritus. But never, never, so long as I have breath in my body will I verify a casual reference. It is slavish and worthless labour. And indeed I am not bound to it here, for my reference is not direct. When I first saw that line, I saw it not in any book of Greek verse but quoted in Michelet. He brings it in in connection with *Stupor Mundi*, the great emperor who so nearly wrecked Europe, and you may say also if you like that a volcanic society produced that volcanic Frederick II, and that he lies there in his porphyry tomb in congenial surroundings. Then there are the dead volcanoes of Auvergne. They have produced no verse that I know of or, if they have, they produced such verse so long ago that it has died as all things die. But the highest among them overlooked the fight at Gergovia and the episode of Vercingetorix is bound up with them. And as for the volcanic Euganean hills, their castles cradled one of the oldest and one of the greatest dynastic families in Europe, from whom also the Guelphs are directly descended; for the Guelphs are only Guelph by adoption. Their German name came from an heiress. They are really Estes.

*　　*　　*

Do not despise the volcanoes of Auvergne or of Este because they are dead, nor for that matter the volcanic lakes of Tuscany and Latium; for there is in truth no such thing as a dead volcano. Volcanoes only slumber, and they mutter in their sleep. Perhaps they never die. Pliny had a startling reminder of this (and has left his account of it) when a volcano, which was thought to be as dead as mutton or as the Puy de Dôme to-day, suddenly shook itself and woke up, roaring horribly and doing devastating things, but preserving antiquity for us in the two examples of Herculaneum and Pompeii. And that volcano, having woken up, has not gone to sleep again. You may see the smoke still curling from it when you look over the plain towards it from the height of Naples: for it is called Vesuvius.

So much for volcanoes—though I see no end to the theme. Why not connect the activity of Japan with its volcanoes?

I may perhaps be blamed here for ascribing such powers to something which is not to be found here

in England: they are "Un-British"—a dreadful thing
to say of any man, beast, or thing. Not even Anglo-
Saxon. For there is none that I know of in the States
(outside Alaska) or Australasia. At the best one or
two are imperial. Volcanoes are alien, they are foreigners, and therefore, I suppose, to be despised.
But still, as foreigners go, they take a high place, and
now that my mind has been started upon their trail,
I shall follow it up.

Ah! me. Would I had spoken of Cotopaxi or
Popocatapetl, whose names alone are worth the
money! But I have come to an end.

The Dead City

I⊤ is a difficult thing to write A Wanderer's Notebook when the wanderer cannot wander, or may only do so under heavy restrictions. If we do not look out (and by "we" I mean Europeans, the civilised men of the West) we shall get so unused to any travel, to any useful travel, to any illuminating and inspiring travel, that the value of it will go out of our minds. Travel was the food for the mind of writers and thinkers (and a good many others) all through that happier period which our cycle of war threatens to end. The men who make the soul of a society, the men who have enough leisure to observe and move, but not so much as to be wasted on luxuries and frivolities, got their chief sustenance during the nineteenth century, from travel. That is what we mean when we say that the cultivated middleclass were the makers of European society. If the gap in their experience lasts much longer the effect of that experience will be lost. It will become a ghost and the life will have gone out of it.

Of my own innumerable memories of travel one of the strongest is indeed of a strange sort; for it is almost anonymous; it hardly relates to any known name or to a known place. It is only the memory of a great plain lying at the foot of mountains against a southern sea; a plain once populous and wealthy, now almost deserted; the flat land only a few miles

in breadth between the huge Corsican mountains and
the Tuscan Sea.

*   *   *

I came upon it many years ago by a sort of accident. I found n.yself in Corte, in the north middle of
Corsica, on my way between the two main ports,
Ajaccio and Bastia. Corte ought to have been enough
to keep a man for days. For it is a mountain town, a
sort of capital of the hills, though very small for such
a part; and it has a seal set upon it: it has a physical
feature which is most memorable, a sort of astonishing Acropolis. This is a precipitous rock actually
overhanging the little city like a breaking wave; a
place which would have made a man's mouth water
in the very early days when men sought out impreg-
nable positions on which to build their lairs. Whether
it ever had been so used for a castle in the past I do
not know, for I was not bothering myself with any
guide-book or reading of any sort.

Well, I found myself in Corte, but I did not linger
there as I should have done. It is the business of those
who desire to live fully to move on and move on
and move on. So from Corte I moved on by a moun-
tain-way, leading me to the east and to the south.
The summer air was heavily scented with that peculiar heath these hillsides produce. It was the enduring
memory of Napoleon. He spoke of it passionately in
his last years, for that scent was the air of his childhood. It was on the second day (had I been younger
I could have done it in one) that I came to the last

lift of the land below which the plain lay spread out before me and the sea beyond. It was the last ridge or spur of those central heights which make up the island. There are two of them, and they join together so that Corsica as a whole may be said to be the coast at their feet with one transverse way on which Corte itself stands.

The flat at my feet was not extended; there were but a few miles, three or four perhaps, five at the most, between the last height on which I stood and the motionless sea to the east. I was filled with a persuasion that this semi-circular sweep of plain between the heights of the shore had been filled in the past with greatness; great wealth, great commerce, great numbers of men, great buildings and generations of memory. But though it is my custom to read these things up when I get home and discover the full meaning of what I have seen abroad, I do not remember ever to have inquired upon the past of that magic emptiness. A sort of shallow mere or marsh, which may have been the relics of a former great harbour, now quite untenanted, took the light of evening from behind the mountains as I gazed. I thought I could make out a lump of ruin on the fringe of this lagoon in the middle distance. For the rest, there was nothingness. There was not even the cry of sea birds.

*   *   *

Surely this opportunity for landing, and, in happier times, for tillage must have been used by the men

who colonised the Western Mediterranean, coming
we know not whence; the first human beings to lay
the foundations of that glorious culture. Surely there
must have been here some main port and on the flats
around it a vigorous small state attached to the
sacred city of the harbour land. But all had died. I
had even to imagine the ghosts. What had happened?

Time telescopes up when one considers antiquity
and emptiness such as this. The whole thing might
have been abandoned yesterday—or thousands of
years ago. To-day it did not attempt to rise again. It
lay there at evening and in silence making part of
the silence and of the evening; saying, as it were, no
more than this: "I was and now am no more. Leave
me to repose." . . .

*   *   *

I hope it is not a paradox (for paradox is a literary
form I avoid as much as possible), but it does seem to
me that the emptinesses of this world help to nourish
the mind: though perilously. They people themselves with the unseen. They are the outliers of Another Country: hence, I suppose, the way they have
of attracting hermits and the reception they have
given to the prophets and the background they form
for revelations. They are the scenes of vision. Therefore, though that Corsican memory is still dreadful,
I cherish it.

The Ogre

A MAN said to me once: "Do you like tripe?" I did
not know who he was, and he did not know me from
Adam. We met by chance in the Jura, and I never
saw him again. I suppose people talk thus in such
chance encounters because they feel secure and cut
off from the world by travel, and are confident that
they will not be recognised again.

Anyhow, that is what he said to me: "Do you like
tripe?"

I answered: "I don't avoid it as much as some
people do, because I find that there is always some
fun to be got out of the more intensely stupid or
ignorant passages, especially when the tripe is historical tripe." But he said in his turn that he was not
talking of tripe literary but of tripe edible, and before
I could deal with that shock he was going on inde-
pendently of any reply I might make: "As a rule,
you know," he said, "it is like eating so much warm
indiarubber; and yet—" (here a look came into his
eyes—an impersonal look as of reminiscence and affection, disconnected with the man he was talking to
and the things he was saying) "—every now and then
as I go on so wearily through life I do find tripe
cooked to perfection. But it needs constant watching, and conscience in the cook as well as patience,
pertinacity and strength of will.

"The most remarkable tripe I ever ate was given
me by an Ogre. He kept a very large hotel in a part

of Europe to which nobody goes because it is not
very picturesque, there is no deep snow, there are
no springs or anything, and the town in which that
hotel stands is a manufacturing town. I had come in
after dusk and had taken to this rather forbidding
large hotel in despair of finding anything better,
when the man who was owner, manager, and everything else appeared to receive me and proved to be,
as I have said, an Ogre. No doubt he was under eight
foot high, but he looked at least that, and he was
broad for his height. He had a very deep, fierce voice,
and the hair bristled on his head and all over his face.

*   *   *

"You must know," said my chance and momentary
acquaintance, "that I can't bear noise. I can't sleep
unless I have absolute quiet. I asked the Ogre rather
timidly whether he had any particularly quiet rooms.

" 'You've come to the right house for that,' he
said, 'and to the right man! I can't understand how
modern people are so foolish as to tolerate noise. All
the top floor of this house, on which floor I live
myself, is made sound-proof with cork walls and
double doors with indiarubber round the edges. You
shall have two rooms on that special floor of mine
and you will find that you can sleep.'

"The Ogre was as good as his word, and showed
me those remarkable rooms. He then asked me what
I would eat, saying that if I were wise, I would take
certain tripe which he had been cooking that very
day with science and care.

" 'There is no tripe like it,' said he, 'in the world, or certainly none that you will ever come across, for not only am I the best of cooks, but tripe is my masterpiece.' You will see by this that he was a boastful Ogre, but indeed braggadocio goes well with Ogres; a timid Ogre is an abomination—out of nature, a contradiction in terms, and several other things.

"I said, of course, that I would be delighted to eat his tripe, and that I was sure it was the best tripe in the world, to which again he briefly answered: 'You are right.'

"It turned out that he had told the truth. That tripe was certainly remarkable, and when he saw that I appreciated it he was pleased in so far as any Ogre can be really pleased, or rather in so far as he can be pleased, knowing that he is pleased; for I have noticed about Ogres this—that they have great zest for life and enjoy themselves more than most of us do, but they are always grumbling and complaining and even roaring their annoyance—that again is the nature of Ogres.

*　*　*

"The Ogre said, as I ate that meal—that excellent, not-to-be-forgotten meal of most exceptional tripe—that it was difficult to get anyone to cook well to-day. He said the art was dying out, and that soon we should end as the beasts of the field, who had to eat their food raw. He also told me why the art of cooking was dying out. He said it was because people were paid not to do work. 'No man or woman can cook,' he said, 'unless he or she loves work, and in particular *that* work. It is arduous work, but it is noble, and earns a great reward. To-day, since they have taken to paying people for not working, every form of craft will die, and cooking has already gone a long way down that road. But not with me!' he said, wagging his great, hairy head, and rolling out the words in monstrous tones, 'Not with me! I can't train lads to cook in my kitchen now, at least, not as they should be trained. Perhaps I don't frighten them enough. They have no pride in their art nor any love for it. All good things are dying,' he went on, with a sigh like a gale in the forest, 'everything gets worse, and there is no remedy,' but he said this with such ferocity that I believe the thought of such a catastrophe was not displeasing to him, ogres, as we know, having of their nature some affinity with the tragic, or, at any rate, the horrible."

*   *   *

He ceased. He was meditating on the Ogre. But he added in a subdued tone:—

"If you want to know how to reach this place I will tell you. You walk down a mountain-side until you come to a very still lake much longer than it is broad, overshadowed by very tall trees. On the shore of this lake you will see a boat and in it standing up, with a paddle in her hand, a goddess of great beauty and quite silent. Ask her to ferry you over the lake; she will nod and do so. When you ask her to take payment on the further shore she will shake her head gently and sweep off again majestically into the waters. Where she leaves you, you will find a small railway station which is a terminus. There you will take the train for the *second* station out, which is the station 'for' that ugly town. In that town you will find the huge, unmistakable hotel, and there in that hotel you will find the Ogre."

"What is the name of the lake and the town," said I, "so that I may find them?"

The Stranger got up and took his hat off the hook.

"That is what I am not allowed to divulge."

He bowed very courteously and disappeared.

On Latin

IT IS a delightful faculty in man that he will always take hold of the wrong end of the stick. The excellent considerations of Mr Chesterton upon that theme will be familiar to my readers.

Man taking hold of the wrong end of the stick with an unfailing instinct for that intellectual attitude shows it particularly in his choice of order. Hearing that he should not murder his grandmother, he will argue for or against. She is a tiresome old woman. She has a lot of money which he could find plenty of use for. Her health has long failed. On the other hand, she makes a dignified figure at the tea table (on the days when she is well enough to come down). She has not yet completed her worthless memoirs. Funerals are expensive.

The two central points: (a) When are we justified in taking human life? (b) Our special responsibilities to our relatives in a certain precedence (more to your grandmother, less to your great-aunt) they will not touch upon.

So it is with that most actual question, the use or disuse of the holy Latin tongue. On the one hand, Latin is a dead language. It takes some time to learn. There are degrees in one's acquaintance therewith, so that however one tries one will suffer the superiority of some greater scholar. It is not commonly understood of the vulgar. It is a language in which exact spelling (especially of the later syllables in any verb,

adjective, or substantive) makes an extraordinary difference which it is indeed difficult to bear in mind:
a difficulty which rendered impatient Gregory Bishop
of Tours. To learn Latin one must employ a teacher,
and that costs money. On the other hand, there is
a certain distinction about knowing Latin. Also you
may, thereby, interpret inscriptions upon public
monuments of the past, and get some idea of what is
meant by familiar quotations such as: *Ne* (or *Nec* or
Non) *plus ultra, Exempli Gratia,* or even *Nisi prius*
and *Floreat Etona.*

But the strongest argument for maintaining Latin
in the education of modern men is that a knowledge
of it, even elementary, adorns one with a cloak of
Mumbo-Jumbo, puts a feather in one's hat, and a
passport to recognition by others as crude as oneself
in the affair. It is true that this last advantage is offset
by the contempt felt for the imperfect Latinist by
anyone even but slightly less imperfect than himself.

The two strongest arguments on the other side are
that in this country, and today, the knowledge of
Latin, even to a very low degree, is confined to men
(and women, alas!) above a certain level of income.
This is very odious to those who feel (as I confess
I do myself) a natural hatred for all those more
wealthy than they should be; that is, more wealthy
than the person contemplating them.

This powerful argument against the learning and
use of Latin especially appeals to those who have no
culture whatsoever, and have thus blared out as
leaders of Modern Thought.

The other argument which is of chief effect for the destruction of Latin among us, is the manifest truth that it is very different from our own tongue, manifestly destined idiom of the whole world. This last truth, then, I say, none will dispute; for in the first place, English is the language which was made in England, and is therefore the premier language of the world. Secondly it enables one to travel throughout Australasia, the United States of America, nearly all Ireland, without interruption, and is accepted without too much difficulty by the head porters of large hotels everywhere, especially those called Palaces.

Yet there are also strong arguments in favour of continuing, for some few at least, an elementary instruction in that Antique fossil called Latin.

They are arguments which have not the weight, I admit, to carry conviction with the majority of readers. They will hardly appeal to the happy millions who depend upon our vigorous contemporary fiction. They will be of no effect upon that main body which feeds upon murder-stories. None the less they are to be considered.

Thus let it be remembered that out of Latin all we of the West proceeded. I know—or at any rate think it probable—though my only authority is at second hand—that many of our ancestors in Christendom began with other kinds of conversation, such as the 132 Slav dialects, the 58 Teutonic, and the lesser number (which for the moment escapes me) of what are called "Celtic"; not to mention the various Negro

idioms, or Lapp, Basque, and Yiddish. But there did
override them all west of the Adriatic and the Car-
pathians and the Marshes of Pinsk, a common priority
of Latin. It formed our philosophers, our grammar-
ians, our lawyers, and even some proportion of our
poets, let alone our pedants, who come to more than
all the rest combined.

The use of this ancient jejune but precise tongue,
bound us of Western Christendom together, and all
that from which we came was steeped in Latin. For
let it be remembered also, that until the advent of
Enlightenment and Progress, Latin was open to all
classes of society. It was discovered in the village
schools, and—shameful it is to say!—boors would pro-
ceed to the very universities themselves until not so
long ago. Nay, to this day in Scotland and other out-
lying places Latin is imparted gratis to the sons of
peasants and artisans.

Which leads me to a further consideration that
Latin is the liturgical language of a considerable religious body, and has enshrined in it not a few theses
and definitions of that body's doctrines.

It is true that all religion has now arrived at such
a stage of decay that it may be called obsolescent (or,
by those who object to Latin "on its last legs"). Yet
during the remainder of its tottering life (the life of
religion, I mean) Latin will remain a necessity, for
the ministers at least, of one sect among us. True, this
can be remedied by a simple reform: the putting of
all common acts of worship into the dialect of each
district, Walloon Romanch, Double-Dutch, Eskimo

or whatnot. That would take some time and might perhaps, in the case of the Creeds, give rise to controversy. For the moment it would seem advisable that some considerable opportunity should be afforded for the acquirement of the Latin tongue; at any rate, in that form which became general after the fourth century of our era. For I admit that too ambitious an aim at the Ciceronian, the Erasmic, the Canine, and other special modes of Latin may do more harm than good. Of this I am convinced by the example of a schoolfellow whose latinity after long study and practice became such that he could not construe what he, himself, had written but a little while before.

Yet other advantages in the knowledge of Latin might be advanced to support its continued study in a few academies. Thus there is the use of it for medical prescriptions, for the writing of palindromes, and especially the nomenclature of new flowers, such as appear annually in the exhibitions opened by ladies, gentlemen and others.

But I have said enough, nay too much, as is commonly the fate of those who come within a mile of the classics.

On the Future of English

THE INHERITANCE of the English tongue is the greatest inheritance we have. People hesitate to believe this because the thing is not visibly and tangibly great, but even more because it does not stand outside ourselves. It is part of us. Yet it is true that the language bequeathed to us is, of all the things we have, the most essential for our posterity and for our own name. It is even more important than the English landscape.

An idiom is primarily the expression of a community; but it is also formative of a community, and especially is it preservative of a community. A language having been formed and its literature cast in one mould the soul of a people has taken on a body, and though that body cannot be immortal—for nothing human is—yet it can be of a vast longevity: of a far longer life than has the community itself. This is particularly true of national verse, which does more than prose for the preservation and fixing of a national language in one form. To preserve his language which has come from the past, to prevent its sterilisation from mere repetition, but much more to prevent its dissolution, is as much the duty of a citizen as is the defence of the soil, and in a sense it is a greater duty, for its effects are more permanent. The language of a people outlives their political form, and testifies to them even after they have dis-

appeared as a separate group among the changing
groups of this world.

*   *   *

Now the English language is threatened to-day in
more than one way.

It is threatened through its ubiquity. It has spread
through commerce and finance and colonial effort
over the whole globe, but it has not spread in any
united fashion. It has settled geographically over
wide areas, so far as the use of the daily tongue is
concerned. It has settled in quite another way,
morally, over certain areas of thought and expression
through the English political genius, and through
English institutions—greatly modified though these
have become outside England.

This universality of English has come to mean not
the universality of one tongue but, in fact, the loose
spreading of various dialects which may (in less time
than we now imagine) become separate languages.
There is hardly any intimate communion of speech
left among the disparate provinces wherein English
of one kind or another is used. Even those accidents
which help to spread the use of English (the cinema
is the most obvious example) distort and weaken the
tongue, and by making it too common make it less
itself.

It is threatened through the daily Press, which is
almost everywhere (but not quite everywhere) concerned with something other than exactitude and
purity of speech. Outlandish words are used because

they are short and fit into headlines. Set phrases are used over and over again, because hurried composition (mostly rushed through at night) falls of its own weakness into set phrases.

These set phrases (of which Stevenson said that they ought all to be cast in one line of type and kept standing for perpetual use) weaken and degrade the tongue, because the essence of any language is a subtle exactitude in the expression of emotion, and set phrases are the enemy and opposite of that.

*   *   *

Meanwhile English is subject, as every other language has been from the beginning of recorded human speech, to the good and evil of mere growth. And here it is that note must be taken of two great examples from antiquity: Greek and Latin.

Greek in literary form remained sufficiently itself to be one recognisable idiom for two thousand years. Modern Greeks have told me that it survives to this day. Certainly it did survive with fixity and hard edges right on until the fall of Byzantium, for there remained until the fifteenth century, I believe, the forms of verse, especially epigrammatic verse, which had begun long before our era.

Latin, on the other hand, went through a very interesting transformation. What we call classical Latin, the Latin of the Augustan period, was perhaps not a generally spoken language—rather a literary language—but certainly by the time of the Vulgate, 400 years later, there had come a transformation.

There had arisen a popular Latin which you find especially crystallised or fossilised in the Scriptures. You discover a change in the meaning of words, e.g. "castellum" for "village"; and you find a change in construction—"quia" coming to be used almost exactly as we use the word "that" in modern English. The order of the sentence also grew modern, and there had come over the finer part of the language that strange influence of rhyme which we have kept ever since—unless indeed modern experiments are destined to destroy it in the English tongue (but I for my part believe that English verse will in the main continue to be rhyming verse).

When all that change had come over Latin, the language crystallised and became what is called a dead language. It was used habitually not only in documents of every kind, including private letters, but in learned conversation right on until the seventeenth century. But vernacular languages arose side by side with it, and supplanted it. During the Dark Ages when the universal Latin of the West slipped into being Provençal and Castilian and Catalan and Portuguese and the Langue d'oc and Langue d'oil and the Tuscan and the Piedmontese and the speech of the Romane Cantons and all the rest of it (even Rumanian), there went on a sort of fermentation on which we have few documents and very little knowledge. But at any rate we know this, that Latin did not survive and seemingly could not survive as a common living tongue among the populace.

It would seem then, from experience, that a tongue spread over many peoples and places may have one of two fates. It may survive unchanged as did Greek, or it may split into a host of separate tongues.

Now which of these two fates awaits English?

The English River

WHEN A man is asked the mark of England he will answer, as a rule, "The sea." But there is something else more permanently and necessarily the physical mark of England, and that is the English river.

For England has had varying fortunes in regard to the sea, the country has been sometimes made by the sea through long periods, and then again betrayed by the sea; for the sea has brought those who raided and ruined England. Sometimes for centuries the sea, which has united England with the ends of the earth, has cut off England from the sources of her life and very nearly put an end to her history.

But by the English rivers England has always been characterised and nourished. There has been no interruption to their necessary and beneficial action, and it can be said of them as cannot be said of the other rivers of Europe, that they actually make the land. The island, that part of it which is fruitful and established, was brought into being as a society by its rivers, whereby commerce and travel reached everywhere. For water carriage was and is by far the easiest, and, until the railway came, the only transport for the great bulk of merchandise. It has been called "a road that moves of itself", and that character the strong tides of our waters increased and emphasised.

Look at the other islands of Europe and see how they lack this principle. Neither Sicily nor Crete nor

Cyprus has a river system. The lands on the Continent
have great rivers each with a system of its own as we
have, but rivers have not given them their unity,
whereas the English rivers formed by their action a
special province in Christendom through their continuous ramifications and their full penetration of the
land, their scores of harbour mouths; nearly all ancient English ports are river ports.

*   *   *

I made many years ago a map, taking for the basis
of it one of those outlines in which every waterway
is set down. On each I marked the first bridge up-
stream from the sea—for it is these "lowest bridges"
which divide the inland river traffic from the maritime. Then I marked above this first bridge the highest point to which a vessel could carry with the tide
if it drew as much as, say, six feet; which is about
the maximum draught of those old pilot-cutters which
were free of every sea and could take any passage at
will and yet also enter the rivers. Then I marked, as
best I could (it was a long task) what was presumably
the highest point to which a loaded boat could reach,
a boat full of armed men or of smaller river merchandise.

When I had done all this, I shaded that area south
of the Border which was bounded by the upper limits
of such river navigation. It was remarkable how little
of the island remained thus shaded, cut off from water
traffic. Even the Cumberland mountains and the
Welsh are flanked and supported by a certain system

of rivers whereby *some* carriage can be done and—
what is important—these provide harbours at their
mouths. As for the Pennines, a larger group which
water traffic cannot serve, the Trent sweeps round
them so as to bring such traffic to either side of the
lower country to the East as well as to the West of
the central range, so everywhere the inland places
could be reached by water.

The ancients said that Gaul was a great example of
providential rivers building up a countryside; but it
would have been far truer to have said it of Britain
south of the Border, south of the Wall. For Gaul had
no river system in its central mountains, and its two
longest rivers were difficult for transport; the Loire
and the Rhone are either too uncertain or too rapid.
But the English rivers (except the upper Severn) go
everywhere, are the social utility which made them
the framework of the country.

*   *   *

Yet the people of the island seem hardly to have
worshipped their rivers. There was some awe attached
to the Dee, and Thames was (rather artificially, I
think) made a sort of god very late in the story, an
imitation, I imagine, of the river-gods of the South,
notably Father Tiber. The English rivers played no
very great part in the songs of the island people either,
and (what is odd!) they were not commonly boundaries. Thames was a boundary, and so was the very
short Mersey, but it was the marshes that made
Mersey a boundary more than the stream. For the

rest our rivers were used occasionally for demarca-
tion, being convenient lines, but they did not as a
rule separate state from state. Even the Severn was
not, as it might have been, the limit of the Mountain
people to the west from the Logrians to the east, and
Trent was still less of a frontier except at the Humber
estuary.

Nor did the rivers of England build up provinces
peculiar to themselves. There was nothing like Anjou,
or like the Normandy of the lower Seine, or the
Gascony of the Garonne. I cannot remember any
group of legends threaded together by one stream
doing for its fortresses and shrines what the Rhine
has done, and yet there is no country remaining of
which the traditional civic life has been more dependent upon its rivers than England. There are a score
of ancient towns in England—more perhaps—which
you recall at once in connection with their rivers.

Lincoln stands as it does because it stands above its
sluggish stream and Durham stands as it does because
its Peninsular Rock has the Tees running round it.
The two universities of England were river universities, and, above all, London is a river town. Of
course, all towns of any size—or nearly all—must be
riverine, but ours were peculiarly so, and to this day,
to most places, to nearly all unspoilt places, the
proper approach is by river. It is one of the things
we have lost in the last hundred years, and one of
the things we should be wise to seek again is the
approach by water, though not, it is to be hoped, by
the aid of the internal combustion engine which, on

board a boat, is death to rivers even more than it is
to roads. For there is a violent contrast and violent
conflict between the majesty of a river, its silence,
its dignity of movement, and the monstrous ham-
mering of petrol, its inhuman speed.

*   *   *

There were till lately—perhaps there still remain—men who explore England and learn her by
way of her rivers. I know that I did so in those distant days when I had leisure to live. Twice did I
cover all Thames from where first it will carry a
canoe well above Lechlade to the sea reaches, and
the little inland rivers were discoveries for me everywhere. There is no better way of tasting the ground
whereon we move during our little passage through
daylight.

Therefore, if you live near a river worship it and
make it your companion. It will remain; its friend-
ship will be for life and will outlast you: a companion. So with me is Arun still.

On Horsemen

THE LEARNED assure us (not that one can always trust the learned) that the horse came late into human life. It is always a relief to believe what is pleasant, though it is more important to believe what is true, but as we do not know what is true in this matter let us lean to the pleasanter hypothesis and believe that the horse and the man have been companions from the very beginning of time. If they have not, so much the worse for them, or, at any rate, so much the worse for the man. The horse does not care: in which he resembles the sailor (another wandering beast).

The learned, I say, assure us that the horse came in among us of the West in the turn between the Mesopotamian preponderance over the ancient world and the Egyptian. They say that the Egyptians knew nothing of the horse until the umpteenth century B.C.—say 4,000 years ago. They also say that when he came in he only came in as a harnessed animal to gallop with chariots into battle; he certainly appears so in early Egyptian frescoes, and much later in the Homeric poems. So be it. I have no quarrel with the learned. If they say it is so, why then so be it.

But the horse must have come from somewhere, and, what is more, someone must have saddled him and bridled him and trotted him about (or, rather, to be accurate, not trotted, for trotting is an artificial pace, but rather loped him or galloped him).

*　　*　　*

Very well then. If the horse came from the East, and was first used in the West for drawing heroes on chariots into battle, well that, at any rate, is better than nothing. And there came a time when even we of the West rode about on him proudly, thinking as we did so what fine fellows we were. Ever since we began doing that the horse has been the companion of man's pride—and what greater service can be rendered by any beast than to give us poor humans some confidence in ourselves? Heaven knows we need it! So true is this that there is a whole set of religions, philosophies, points of view, cultures, and I don't know what and all, the main business of which is to fill us with confidence.

Well, then, the horse, in so far as we ride upon him and move him around, is I say, most serviceable, and we are, or should be, most grateful to him.

We have put up statues to horses, as we do to no other creature. There are, indeed, statues of other animals of all kinds all over the world, notably of lions, and of innumerable elephants; but of the horse men make a special study, almost a portrait. The reason is they say to themselves: "We men can look very grand on a horse, but how silly we look when the mount is deficient." Hence the fine statues of horses.

As for the Frieze of the Parthenon, it is most lively, but they seem to me not to be horses but ponies, on which account—I mean the small stature of the beast—the human being rides him with the greater ease. Our fathers were wont to distinguish between those who rode the smaller and the greater horse, praising the exceptional men (such as Cranmer) who were expert in the management of the latter. It is worth noticing, by the way, that the races most famous for their horsemanship have ridden quite small mounts. Such were the Mongols; such, for the most part, the Arabs. And that brings to my mind another matter—the stirrup.

Whether we got the stirrup from the East, as we are said to have got the horse, I know not—nor do the learned. At any rate, there is no representation of the stirrup before the end of the Roman Empire, I believe, in the West. It may very well be, as I once read in a book, that the stirrup came in from Asia with the migrations along the North of the Black Sea. When it did come in, it raised this very interesting point: does your true horseman ride with a short stirrup or a long? There is a whole tradition on the continent of Europe, emphasised by the mounted men of the French wars (from at least the Crusades onwards), that it is disgraceful to ride with a short stirrup. "If you ride with a short stirrup," they say, "you are not sitting your horse, you are being carried about by your horse. You are an armchair rider. You are not a captain, you are a passenger." To which I can imagine the Mongol and the Arab replying from their respective deserts: "We know more about it than you! We lived on horseback for centuries before you were born or thought of. The horse was our familiar when you were wearing the skins of wild beasts and living in huts. We have always ridden with the shortest stirrup conceivable. We almost kneel as

we ride; and every other fashion seems to us an undue
burden upon the beast and an undue inconvenience
and jolting to ourselves."

*   *   *

I am assured by those of my friends who still ride
horses (whether in pursuit of the fox or of fashion,
or futility that also begins with "f") that Englishmen
have long been divided between these two opinions.
One of my friends at least told me that he shortened
the stirrup only when he felt fatigued at the end of
a day's work. It is not for me to judge. But I know
this: that riding without any stirrups at all (of which
in my early youth I did more than a little) does at
least teach one to sit a horse, though it does not give
one a graceful appearance.

Now I cannot leave the subject of horsemanship
without casting back for a moment to the great name
of Hector. It is wise to call him in verse "Hector the
horseman". But I suppose the real meaning of the
epithet "Hippodamoios" is much more "horse-
breaker" than "horseman", though no one would
like to allude to the great Hector as a mere horse-
breaker. It is too near "horsecoper" for dignity. Anyhow, Hector and horses go together, not only because
they both begin with an "h", but because "hero"
also begins with an "h"; and I will leave it at that.
There is a line which a great many people know by
heart and which I hope I shall never forget, even in
the extremes of age. I have quoted it far too often,
so I shall quote it here again. It is a line in which the

horse appears once more (by allusion): the last line of the great poem:

Thus went they about the tomb of Hector, the tamer of horses.

He went unaccompanied out of this world, and he died on foot, because Phoebus Apollo left him—a dirty trick. But I can believe that in the better places he has a horse to stroke and to feed.

On Port

I HAD already set this title down long ago for a medi-
tation when a sacred fear seized me, for I knew that
I was approaching holy ground. I return to it now
reluctantly not with temerity but with awe and trem-
bling. Port is an adopted son of England, and anyone
who attacks him is attacking the family—a formidable
enterprise. Anyone who praises him may by some
slight overpraise or misjudged praise give even more
offence than by open attack. It is always so with family things: better keep out of them.

*   *   *

Of foreign things which are also modern (meaning
by modern that which we came to know after the
renewal of England in the seventeenth century) Port
comes earlier than Tea, and it seems to me at least to
have a nobler lineage, for it is of Christendom,
whereas Tea is of Cathay. The name of the town,
Oporto, means no more than "the port", and when
they talked of Oporto wine and then shortened it
into Port they were getting back to the English form
of the Latin word for harbour, which English form
had come in its turn from the French form of the
Latin word *Portus*, as one should say a "he-door",
just as *Porta* is a "she-door". A port was the gate into
and out of a country. That, if I remember aright, was
one of the arguments in favour of the Crown during
the violent quarrels of King and Parliament before

the Civil Wars. I will not risk my memory upon the occasion of the quarrel when this argument turned up. I seem to remember it was Bates's Case. But anyhow the reasoning was that the King had a right to say what should come in and out of the country by its ports because the ports were the gates of the kingdom, and a man would not be master in his own house unless he had control of the doors thereof. So here you have the word "port" come home again in quite a different sense, and used to represent quite a different thing from what it had done till those few generations ago.

When a man said, "I hope to make port," everyone up to a certain date knew what he meant; he could only mean one thing; it was a sentence that could only have been spoken either at sea or in prospect of a sea voyage. But after that date a man saying, "I hope to make port," might mean one of two totally different things. He might mean, "I hope to reach harbour," or he might mean, "I hope by the use of chemicals to produce something sufficiently like portwine to deceive the vulgar."

You could not have two phrases with more dissimilar meanings! And all because the old word "port" having taken a long circular flight came to roost again on another branch.

It is so with many another word, "stuff", for instance, and "rout"; and a delight it is (to me at least) to follow verbal gyrations and transformations of that kind. "Stuff" began with the wad of tow or whatnot which was soaked in oil and stuck into the narrow necks of great jars to prevent the wine going sour. Then it wandered about and came to mean "cloth", and then "matter", then it branched off and hooked arms with "nonsense"; then it turned into a verb and meant filling. It hasn't done yet. It still has far to go and many a summerset to turn.

As for "rout", it came from "déroute", which meant being driven off your "route" or road, and that word "route" comes according to the learned Wiener from the Assyrian for a postal system. But I am getting tired of all this digression, and I must make for Port again.

*   *   *

Though I know nothing essential of Port (and that is why I am writing on it), yet I have, like the rest of my fellow citizens, a certain empiric or experimental acquaintance with it. I have drunk a glass of it from time to time, and I have seen strange things happen in connection with it. For instance, a friend of mine (it is now forty years ago) said to me, as he pulled the cork out of a bottle, "I have here some very remarkable port which came from my grandfather; it is of the year so-and-so" (mentioning a date before the Flood), "and I have kept it specially for this occasion." I thanked him as in duty bound. Then with the gesture and expression of one performing a high religious rite he let loose imprisoned Bacchus from his spongy door. But on the appearance of the god, the god had changed complexion and had even changed his very nature. For in colour he came out like dirty milk and in taste like nothing on earth. My friend said "It has passed its prime." Anyhow, there is no doubt that this Port, as Port, had ceased to function. It was "defunct" in the fullest and the most absolute sense of the term.

Then, also, I have been given as Port under alien stars something which was about as much like Port as rice rolled in blacking is like caviare. This strange foreign Port which has appeared before me like an evil vision in town after town, from Cracow to Canyon City, always turned up in a new garment of its own. It has always borne some hitherto quite unknown and, to me, fantastic label. But that does not only apply to Port, that matter of labels, and it works both ways, I mean an absurd label may be attached to an exceedingly good bottle of wine.

I have an example of this in my memory, when, in the first year of the Great War, a hostess asked me whether I would tell her what I thought of a certain wine. She brought this wine. It was a white wine and bore a label on which was printed the simple words *Mes Amours*. I confessed that the vintage was unfamiliar to me, as also the label, which was surrounded with a lot of little dancing Cupids linked together by a ribbon. But when I came to drink this wine it was a really good Montrachet. Now how did a really good Montrachet get into a bottle with a label like that? I cannot tell you. It is one of the myriad mysteries with which we are surrounded from

the cradle to the grave; and as for any man who denies
mystery, let him be anathema—and a donkey to boot.

*   *   *

I have far from exhausted (I am not quite sure if
these last five words are good English), anyhow I am
far from having exhausted my superficial and very
provincial acquaintance with Port, but I will squeeze
in one last tale about it here. A deservedly famous
connoozer of Claret, *jam senex* (the connoozer, not
the wine) was offered some Port by a much younger
man and when he had tasted it was asked what he
thought of it. He answered, "It's all alcohol to me!"

With this immortal phrase I leave you. I am not
sure that I have not printed that story before, but it
is worth printing thousands of times and distributing
throughout the human race.

The Great Sea-Serpent

I SHOULD very much like to see the Great Sea-Serpent;
but what we desire and what we obtain are things so
different that I fear I shall never set eyes on it. And
yet he has been seen, yes and by mortals, and upon
many occasions. He was seen off Beachy Head many
years ago and he has been seen all over the place;
for it is his advantage that he has the ocean for his
field. Even when he turned up in Loch Ness the
other day he took the precaution of choosing a spot
which could be reached from the open sea. He scorns
to be thought a land lubber.

The Great Sea-Serpent has this invincible advantage over all other animals: that he has passed himself
off for a myth. That, by the way, is a special boon to
me in writing of him as I am now doing. For were I
writing of any other rare but recurrent visitant, I
should have to look up dates and references and all
manner, lest the learned or the merely cantankerous
should come a hunting of me. But as nobody believes
in the Great Sea-Serpent (at least hardly anybody) I
can treat him with comfortable contempt. In this he
resembles the Unicorn; though I remember having
read (in a newspaper of all places!) that there had
been discovered in Asia the skull of a unicorn with
the horn well and truly screwed on for the confusion
of sceptics. But then the whole thing may have been
a plant, like the lost Books of Livy at Naples—you
never can tell.

* * *

Although the Great Sea-Serpent has succeeded in passing himself off as mythical—that is, as non-existent, fabulous and in general to be ridiculed by all half-educated men and by most educated men as well—I note that he has managed to give himself certain fixed characteristics, and fixed characteristics are essential to a reputation. If the Great Sea-Serpent had appeared now as a hippopotamus, now as a thing with many legs, now as a thing with large wings; if it had been gifted with speech or even with song, the contemptuous neglect of him would have swollen out of all knowledge. Men would have said, "So unstable a beast can have no real existence. Unity is the first principle of being." And even the most impossibly modern and ignorant of them would have quoted Aristotle to that effect. But the Great Sea-Serpent knew his business. On the rare occasions when he deigned to manifest himself, he never failed to have certain fixed principles which render him worthy of respect and justify his local habitation and his name. The first of these is that he undulates (from *unda*, a wave). One may argue that this undulation is merely the waggling of a long neck. Such is the tenet of the great Cervical School, better called the Corporeal or Torsic (if that is the word I want), which stoutly maintains that the Great Sea-Serpent (so-called forsooth!) is not a serpent at all, but a kind of monstrous swan or duck, the main body of which is commonly hidden beneath the waters, only projecting its neck above the element it lives in, like man striving fitfully for some glorious moment of Beatitude. But an opposing school of thought (which may more simply be called the Serpentine) maintains that there is no great swollen body but that the whole thing is neck; or neck and tail combined. The discussion has, so I understand, raged so passionately that the learned professors of the one school will not speak to the learned professors of the other; and when, by unhappy accident, they meet at some learned assembly they come to blows, or at the least scratch each other's faces.

At any rate, all are agreed that whether it be only a part of him or all of him, the Great Sea-Serpent deigns to appear to mortal men as a rule in a long thin waggling shape, and some of his votaries, who are weak in logic, appeal to his very name as a proof that he is a snake and nothing more than a snake.

*   *   *

But there is another constant feature in the dear beast. He has a head and he always swims in the direction of his head. He allows his head to lead, which shows him to be more sensible than most human beings. And there is a third thing about him which never changes, or hardly ever: he has hair. In this again he shows great cunning. For whereas most serpents differ from the rest of the popular fauna in being quite bald and as smooth and hairless as an egg, the Great Sea-Serpent is usually seen with so much hair along the ridge of him that it has even been called a mane.

Other constant marks he has none that I know of, so they will not badger him about them when he tries for a passport, but it is surely remarkable that he does maintain so consistently a special character: and it is greatly to his honour. I might add one more. Nearly always when he appears he moves very rapidly. That is because he does not show up until he has been disturbed. His natural habitat is in the depths of the salt, like Thetis; and I take it that he would not leave those majestic, those silent, those dark recesses unless he had been shocked by an earthquake.

* * *

The Great Sea-Serpent had this great value in philosophy; that he is a test of scepticism. I do not think he meant to be such, any more than the peacock's tail (which troubled poor Darwin so much) was intended by the peacock to be a poser for the Selectionists. But though he never intended to be a snag for the Confident Doubter, a snag for the Confident Doubter he remains.

For consider carefully this enormous truth: almost everyone in a Confidently Doubting generation laughs the Great Sea-Serpent to scorn. Even to-day when the complacency of our fathers has received many a nasty buffet and is staggering about, the Great Sea-Serpent is almost a by-word for foolish illusion and popular superstition. Yet (as he has himself bitterly complained to a friend of mine) there is no sort of reason to question his existence. Why should there not be a Great Sea-Serpent? or even a little one for that matter? No one can say that the serpentine form is anomalous to sea-water or to liquid of any kind.

On the contrary, nothing lends itself more to worms, eels and long wrigglers of every sort than water, soft or fresh; and as for slime it delights in such. One expects such things in slime, and all are agreed that if the Great Sea-Serpent has a natural bed, its natural bed is slime. As for the argument from his rarity, the same applies to poets, saints, companionable women and good generals, let alone tolerable cooks.

On Clocks and Watches

CIVILISATION LOSES its treasures by an unconscious process. It has lost them before it has appreciated that they were in the way of being lost: and when I say "its treasures" I mean the special discoveries and crafts of mankind which, when they are good enough and numerous enough, we call collectively a "culture" or civilisation.

For instance, we lost—sometime during the twelfth century, it seems—the art of beaching large vessels. Antiquity did it—large Carthaginian armies and the Normans, and there were perpetual allusions in the classics to the beaching of boats. Until 800 years ago big ships carrying whole armies were beached, even in tideless seas. Now, how was it done?

There is one craft which has not gone, but it looks in danger of going. It was a discovery or adaptation made by the men of Western Christendom. This discovery was the mechanical measure of time—the clock and the watch.

We have not lost the art, but we are in the process of losing it through mass production. There are still great watchmakers and great clockmakers, but manifestly the same process which has put watches within the reach of all has made it difficult for the special excellence of the craftsman to compete. And who knows whether, even only a hundred years hence, the chronometer will survive, let alone the common clock?

Electricity can cheaply and universally synchronise all clocks and where there are many public clocks the gaining or losing of a few seconds by a watch is of no great consequence. The watch can always be set right in a moment.

* * *

When the creative power of man had produced its first flowers in this department it revelled, as it always does at the beginning of any creative effort, in its own creative power. The early clockmakers delighted in showing to the world not only the best they could do in their special machinery, but how their effort might be ornamented, diversified, and branched out. We had little figures walking past in procession to mark the hours. We had puppets striking gongs and bells. We had the phases of the moon, the days of the month. All manner of things were marked on their dials. Nothing in my travels has delighted me more than these things which seem to us extravagances but are really witness to Man the Maker. Willingly do I return, always with pleasure, to the great clock of Strasburg which excels in this fashion.

Well, all that is over. I can remember no modern clock, no clock of the nineteenth century (let alone of the twentieth!), that has a host of little mechanical servants at its command to strike the hours, or has any great diversity of function. One might say that the horological zest had faded, that the sacred horological fire had sunk. Perhaps we shall have a renaissance, and there will yet be among clockmakers a

Theocritus from whom shall leap up the many-coloured flame, though the oil in the lamp seem exhausted. I, myself, have seen since the Great War things that relieved my sadness. For instance, I saw a clock in Bond Street which had solved the problem—not, indeed, of perpetual motion in a mechanical sense, but at any rate of uninterrupted function. For what kept it going was the changeable pressure of the air. It was "wound up", if I may so express myself, automatically by the going up and down of the barometer.

But of a love for watches and clocks of that intimate domestic kind without which there is (I beg your pardon) no *poesis* I find to-day no trace.

*   *   *

I know that there are great makers of watches and clocks still creeping and breathing upon this earth, and two within my own acquaintance hand on a family tradition which will make their successors as valuable as they themselves have been.

I have seen the most exquisite workmanship in that only part of the business which I am competent to appreciate, the decoration and caligraphy of the watch and the clock. We have all seen the contemporary and hitherto unfailing accuracy of minute work in England and France and Switzerland, and, indeed, throughout Christian Europe the art has not yet wholly failed. But the making of a timekeeper as the function of an artist and a freeman is not the dominating mark of the craft to-day.

That craft has had a life singularly short as the record of human craftsmanship goes. It grew through stages of experiment and increasing care and skill until the earlier eighteenth century. It became one of the glories of Europe when my great-grandfather was a young man. Its climax continued for another three lifetimes, indeed until the machine-made watch of the later nineteenth century—and now it would seem that its day is nearly ending, its sun near to setting.

Some will reply that the chronometer, which is the perfection of horological man, cannot pass out. I could wish this to be true! Alas, I can only *wish* it to be true! They say the chronometer cannot pass just as they said in the past that the full-rigged sailing ship, that glory of England, was a final achievement which had come to stay for ever.

Well, we have seen the clipper go, and it will not return. That tower of canvas, many storied and alive, leaning, urging through foam, is now a picture or a ghost. It has left the real world. The argument that it must remain has failed.

There is always something left out in such arguments, and that something is the recognition of mortality as a condition universal. Men are so full of themselves that they talk of their own human mortality sometimes (though not enough), but they do not sufficiently appreciate how mortality shades with its vast obscuring wing all things whatsoever, and, among other things, these excellent works of man, watches and clocks.

In vain do you tell me that the chronometer, which is the perfection of horological man, cannot pass out because it is essential to navigation. Is it? I have seen too many essential things die even in my own brief mortality to pin my faith to any one of them.

To-morrow there may come some discovery whereby even my own small boat, which is only ninety-one years old (if you disbelieve this you do so at your peril), may know its longitude wherever it happens to be, and that without reference to any timekeeper on board.

I know not. No man knows. But pray mark this, that all things terrene do pass. You have been warned!

On Proportion

TRUTH LIES in proportion. This is so obvious that one would think everyone could appreciate it at once. You are not telling the truth about any matter if your statement is out of proportion; that is, if it does not put the most important things first and all others in their due place. If someone who has never heard of Bismarck were to ask you who Bismarck was and you were to answer that he was a rather talkative German with gooseberry eyes and a high voice, you would not have told the truth about Bismarck. However small the space allowed you for describing him, you would have to say that he was the first statesman of his day; you would have to give, however roughly, the dates of his activity; you would have to say that he was of the same stature in his own profession as William Cecil, Lord Burleigh or Richelieu. You would have to say that he put his talents to the service of his master, the King of Prussia, and rapidly raised this master to the first place in Europe.

After that you might add in their order any number of other things about him, but you would not be telling the truth if you did not put the first things first; and if you left out the major matters, so as to leave the inquirer ignorant, you would be telling that inquirer a falsehood.

True history is simply history which puts the past in its right proportion. False history is always "put across" by undue emphasis on this or that and by the suppression of this or that which is essential to your narrative. That is why, by the way, most national history is false; because national history is written as though the general events of the world could be referred to the fate of one nation alone, and, on the top of that, national history is nearly always written with the object of exalting the particular nation concerned. False history will usually have a greater effect and a much more lasting one than true history. It will be more interesting through its passion. Wrong proportion here is all to the advantage of literature, but all to the disadvantage of that prime service which history should render—the teaching of men how to conduct the present through experience of the past.

Now, if truth lies in proportion (which I say should almost be self-evident, although it is hardly ever said), it is also true that beauty lies in proportion—and this is much less easy to grasp, for there seems to be no rational connection between the one and the other. Yet so it is; by a blunder in, or an ignorance of, proportion you will always mar beauty and often produce its opposite: the ludicrous, the grotesque, and the repulsive. But why should that be so? Young people hardly ever understand this, or even appreciate it; though, being candid, they feel it. It is rather in age and after too much experience that one looks eagerly for proportion in the works of man and finds repose and satisfaction therein. I suppose the ultimate reason is that beauty must be consonant to creation in general.

There is also in human art a certain element of proportion which consists in its relationship to man; man made it and made it to be enjoyed by man.

Thus the gigantic is never great; the exaggerated always fails of its effect. If a roof be too exalted or a hall too vast, we lose the sublimity of either. I was saying to myself only the other day, in Rome, that the nave of St. Peters seemed to me, with its pendant hollow dome above it, and its immense, but in truth restrained, ornament, just on the limit of what was tolerable in the way of largeness. A little more and the effect would have been missed.

In the same way, Beauvais is just on the extreme of Gothic height. Not that you might not have an ogival arch much higher and of less effect, but that Beauvais, looking up and eastward from the transept at the crossing which the Black Death left for ever unfinished, seems to me, from its exact use of proportion, the highest thing in the world. Yet note that if you were to reproduce that sublime thing to a scale of one half in every dimension of the original, you would produce no such emotion of aspiration and maturity. You would produce something ridiculous. That is because Beauvais was made for man by men. I wonder what dwarfs think of it? I have never asked one.

But speaking of architecture, the true and complete satisfaction of proportion in building is not so much found in the attempt, even the successful one, at expressing an intense emotion, as in the fulfilling of a purpose, and this, for some reason, seems always to be connected with the simplest elements. It has been said that all the great forms are to be found in the first three books of Euclid; the greatest of all is the semi-circle of the perfect arch. The ogive is the intersection of two equal semi-circles, so that its pointed arch exactly contains an equilateral triangle, each side of which is a radius; and the diagonal of the square gives you that subtle and complete satisfaction—the proportion of unity to the square root of two. I suppose there is nothing more completely satisfactory than your mullion window such as you will find it in the best stone work of the Cotswold, and the perfect mullion window has the oblong light surmounted by a square, and the height of that light is the diagonal of the square above or, alternatively, a multiple of the side of the square. I have never found why that particular proportion so completely fills the eye, but it does so.

The conic sections, parabola, and hyperbola, would seem unsuitable to the works of man. Even the ellipse, if it be at all exaggerated, disturbs the eye. Parabolic and hyperbolic curves in architecture merely disturb and offend, and that is perhaps because there is no finality about them. The parabola comes out of infinity and goes back to it again. The hyperbola is an ellipse which has been turned inside-out beyond the boundaries of the real. It is shooting away from reality and is always trying to touch what it never attains. There still stands, I believe, in Barcelona, one of the most hideous buildings in the world, a new cathedral called, by an awful misnomer, "The Holy Family."

In this the eccentric architect prided himself in
avoiding all segments of a circle and making his
doors and his windows parabolic or elliptical. It survived the war. Will it survive the return of sanity to
our civilisation?

Fortitude

IN PERIGUEUX, which is the capital of the Perigord, in
the hill districts of Central France, there is a strange
building: strange, not for its history or for anything
mysterious about it, but for two qualities: its incon-
gruity and its strength without apparent purpose.
This building is the cathedral of Perigueux and of
Perigord.

It is incongruous because being of extremely ancient foundation it is wholly modern in construction,
so that you might think on looking upon it from
within or from without that it had been designed
and accomplished all within some few years of the
nineteenth century. It is incongruous as being something Eastern, though cut off by hundreds of miles
from any Eastern thing. Its roof is in five cupolas (or
seven if you count the smaller ones); they are not
domes; they are essentially Oriental cupolas; they
would not be astonishing near any of those Mediterranean shores which have been affected by the neighbourhood of Mahomedan things. But they are unique
here in the Perigord.

But that other quality of which I have just spoken—
the quality of strength combined wth newness and
unsupported by anything but its own stark self—is
more remarkable even than the exotic lines of the
building. It is built of huge blocks of stone almost
without ornament: great slabs of wall from roof to
ground; great drums of masonry from roof to ground;

and that is nearly all. A man might feel, looking on those exactly squared, precisely sawn, unchiselled stones, that they would never weather. They suggest nothing of tradition. They are one of those French things which hardly even attempt beauty, or if they attempt it fail. Huge blocks, enormously solid, and apparently without story or legend, and almost without meaning. Yet their meaning is profound, and those huge stone blocks are connected with my theme, which is Fortitude.

Inside that cathedral, on a side altar of the northern transept, if I remember right, the undecorated solid bare transept of mere stone (but what stone!), the semi-circular arch, the absence of all detail and of nearly all colour, but the presence of Strength—there stands a mosaic. It is the mosaic of an elephant, rather large as elephants are wont to be. It has a quiet eye and an immovable expression. Under it, also in mosaic, is the word "Fortitudo". And there you are.

*　　*　　*

It has been remarked by men from the beginning of time that chance connections may determine thought: a chance tune heard in unexpected surroundings, a chance sentence not addressed perhaps to oneself and having no connection with the circumstances around, the chance sight of an unexpected building appearing round the corner of a road, the chance glance of an eye that will never meet our eyes again—any one of these things may establish a whole train of contemplation which takes root and inhabits the mind for ever. So it was with me all those years ago in the matter of the elephant of Perigueux and his Fortitudo. Perhaps I remember it better because I was in the company of the wise when I thus came across it for the first and last time.

Fortitude (and her elephant) were here set up in a Christian church because fortitude is entitled one of the great virtues. Now what is fortitude? It is primarily Endurance: that character which we need the most in the dark business of life. But if fortitude be endurance, it is also creative endurance, and at the same time it involves some memory of better times and some expectation of their return. It involves, therefore, fidelity and hope; and, without these two, fortitude would be of little use: but above all fortitude is endurance.

* * *

Fortitude is the virtue of the menaced, of the beleaguered. It is the virtue of those of them that man the wall, or that are called upon to last out, for all extremes; it is the converse to and the opposite of aggressive flamboyant courage, yet it is the greater of the two, though often it lacks action. Fortitude wears armour and holds a sword. It stands ready rather than thrusts forward. It demands no supplement; it is nourished not from without but from within. It is replenished of its own substance. Fortitude does not envisage new things; rather does it tenaciously preserve things known and tried. It builds, but builds

unwittingly, not following an inspired plan nor a
mere vision, but of necessity; and from stone to stone
of daily conservative achievement.

Sometimes fortitude will earn fame, but not often.
Always, however, it will earn reward; for even when
the defensive fails at the end, if it has been of an
efficient sort, it makes an air and a name surrounding
and enshrining itself. So have the great sieges of history done. So will our time to-day, if we use it aright.

* * *

There was a time in the long story of Christendom
(which is also Europe) when fortitude was everywhere
and was known everywhere to be supreme. That time
was the ninth to the tenth century, from the death of
Charlemagne to the awakening which began with
Cluny, continued through the annealed, architectural, legislative, Normans in the South as in the
North, and rose in the flame of the Reconquista and
the enormous march of the Crusades.

Between that darkening and that sunrise lay the
night of Europe, wherein we nearly perished. Then
indeed were we under siege, from the murderous
pirates of the northern seas, from anarchy within and
the failure of law, from the Asiatic Mongol hordes
riding to the Lech and their disastrous battle, even
reaching the Saone for one moment at Tournus. The
Mahomedan, our superior in seamanship and arms,
had mastered all the Levant and Africa. In all the
temper of that time was threat and the imminence of
disaster. Destruction seemed native to it and the air

of defeat: invincible opponents: desperate resistance against odds filled all that was left of our inheritance. There was no respite, no long truce, no relief; only continual battle. There was no support at all save in ourselves nor even any final confidence, and of prophecy hardly any save prophecy of evil and of the end.

Yet we rallied and we conquered. We baptised the pirates when we had tamed them; we recovered Spain; we marched 2,000 miles until we had stormed Jerusalem. We re-established universities; we set up triumphantly the Gothic of the pointed arch. The West rose up again in glory, having been saved by Fortitude.

On Fame

THERE IS nothing in the high comedy of the world so admirably comic as the special department called Fame.

I don't mean comic in the sense that it makes you roar with laughter; I mean comic in the sense that it illustrates the nature of man.

All men desire fame. I have never known a single exception to that rule, and I doubt if anyone else has. I have known a few very holy men who have very nearly got rid of the love of fame; there was left in them no more than a trace of it.

I say that in a few very holy men I have in the course of my life met those who had left in them only a trace of this love of fame. A very much larger number of exceedingly unholy men have I met who had largely lost the love of fame because they were tired out. They had suffered or enjoyed so many emotions; they had seen so many men rise to prominence, often suddenly and as a rule, without any good reason for their elevation; they had felt so many disappointments, rushing after pleasure and nearly always missing it; they had reached such a contempt for their fellow-beings, the mob who are the makers of fame, that they had become in some large measure indifferent.

*　　*　　*

But not altogether! I never yet knew a man so *blasé*

that his face did not change when he heard that some action or creation of his had been praised; yes, even when that praise came from men most insignificant. There is, I believe, but one exception to this and that is the tedium of repeated praise and especially of praise repeated for the wrong reasons. I knew a man once who was a poet of the third or fourth class, being also wealthy. Now this man, like many another wealthy man, indulged as a pastime in the hatred of his own country; which country, I may tell you, was one the citizens of which are given to the most extravagant complacency and self-praise. This man, while he was still quite young, had written one line— only one—in which he expressed strong emotion on seeing once more the shores of his country after long absence overseas. The line was commonplace, vulgar and silly, also alliterative. It, therefore, had great vogue. It appeared in many anthologies. It was the only thing on which he received fan-mail; and young girls used to drive him mad by pestering him to write it down in their autograph books. At last my poet simply could not bear his fame in this one particular and came near to changing his name and flying to the Antipodes.

But for the most part men are especially pleased with praise of their verse, and that is as it should be. For, in the first place, if verse were not praised it would soon dry up. It has already nearly dried up as it is, and it would be a great pity for verse to dry up considering the pleasure it gives to the young.

Certainly verse would not carry on long for the

sake of any profit made out of it. For though occasionally a man does make profit by selling his verse, the excellence of the verse has no more to do with the money value of it than the beauty or majesty of a landscape has to do with the money value of the soil. I suppose the majesty of the desert, seen from the escarpment of the Middle Atlas, covers an area much like that of Greater London. Yet there is no comparison in the ratable values of the two. The French Sahara is emphatically what the late Lord Salisbury well called it, "light soil". But the value of the built-up area between Ealing and the Isle of Dogs, Sydenham and Highgate is considerable—nay, large. Also I did hear one man once say that he thought it beautiful. I don't.

* * *

Fame coming by way of verse is the favourite example, I suppose, because it is the most enduring. Most pieces of great verse have their authorship securely tied on to them, and even the poor mutts who think that the Odyssey was written by a committee of dons have not much longer to live. Well, to have written a great piece of verse is certainly to have acquired an enduring form of fame. The poet usually gets it after he is dead, and it was a wise man who, when he had been asked whether he expected fame for his metrical compositions, replied, "I shall have all the fame a dead man wants."

On the other forms of fame (a long way *after* literary fame) the greatest is military fame. But I have always thought that the pleasure here was a little mixed by the certain knowledge any good soldier has that the thing was not done by his hand alone. There is the quality of the troops; there is their handling of their weapons; there is the aid given by subordinates, and there is the inner knowledge of luck and sometimes, of complete irresponsibility. Many a battle has been won by a disgusting fluke. Then there is this drawback, also, about military fame. That many a man must know he has deserved it, yet not attained it; and there is this further drawback about military fame: even more than fame for verse, it catches on to incongruous and unworthy occasions and men. A first victory after many defeats or doldrums is always the most violently acclaimed. Blenheim was far more extolled than Ramillies. Yet Ramillies was the greater feat of arms, by far. And as for Fabius Cunctator, I certainly can't remember what his last decisive battle was, if any; and I very much doubt if you can. Yet, according to all accounts, he did the trick.

*　　*　　*

Time was when men could acquire fame by holiness; and it still is so, so I am told, in North Africa and the East. Men always acquire fame rapidly by getting hold of a large sum of money, no matter how. Fame is even to be got by a marriage.

Fame can be acquired by anybody who does not distinguish between fame and notoriety. But then, this kind of fame is not really fame at all. Fame can be got by mere purchase (which is a different thing from the fame of sudden fortune). Fame can be got by inheritance, by mistake and even (on very rare occasions) by courage. But there is one quite certain way of acquiring such measure of fame as is suitable to your condition in life whether as a politician or a pork-butcher, and it only requires one advantage—longevity.

This method, which I heartily recommend to everybody with the prospect of a few years of life, is flattery of the young. Be good to the young; but that is not enough. Flatter them. You will soon die, but the young, like our evil deeds, live after us; and in middle age they invariably revere those who praised them in youth. Thus they create a legend. I have never known it fail.

On Innocence

No ONE can understand the value of innocence who does not appreciate its positive quality. The word does not mean (as its derivation might make one think) a mere absence of evil; for there would seem to be no evil in a lump of clay, yet it has no innocence. We predicate innocence of a will which might turn to evil later on, but which has not yet done so. Therefore the word connotes a will in action, but a will in action for good in some degree. And since it is a will in action without any evil intent, therefore it is a will wholly good—though perhaps ill-instructed, as when a young child throws a stick into the spokes of a moving bicycle, or (as happened in a sea-port town the other day) pushes a motor over the edge of a quay into a dock for fun.

Innocence depending thus on the will and being defined by the will, being a quality attached to conscious and moral beings, has a positive quality, and it is this positive quality which is the very core and essence of it.

Our remote ancestry of over 300 years ago expressed their appreciation of this positive character about innocence when they said that it was specially protected, and that it moved unhurt in the midst of danger—an exaggeration. The emotion aroused by the spectacle of innocence, even the aesthetic emotion, apart from the moral emotion, should be very strong in any normal man for there is something

divine about it. Yet you may note that very few creative artists in any art have ever evoked that emotion,
and I suppose the reason is that the creative power
tends to be abused being too much for man to handle,
so that he who could best carve or paint or write or
draw will commonly have lost the faculty for inter-
mixing his mind with that of innocence, and thereby
fully portraying innocence with intimate and lively
knowledge of what it is. He may feel the impact of
innocence from outside; he may admire it and more
or less suggest its externals, but very rarely indeed
will the creative man *reproduce* innocence and give
the reader or the onlooker the same emotion as will
be produced by the presence of innocence itself.

*   *   *

I do not mean by all this that who drives fat oxen
should himself be fat, or that only the innocent can
paint or sculpt or describe or evoke innocence; but I
do mean that there must be some considerable remains of remembered innocence at least in anyone
who attempts the task. The perfectly innocent, of
course, are innocent of art and of everything else,
and good luck to them. Indeed, that is a wasted wish,
for they have all the luck there is, and they have it
all the time, anyhow.

The painters get at it best, and very often a painter
of manifestly corrupt mind will pull it off. Of the
painters whose works I have seen, Botticelli seems to
be the most successful in this line. Never did he
catch innocence with his grown-ups, for he seems to

have chosen the most abnormal of these—even approaching the near cadaverous sometimes. But his younger angels are of a ravishing innocence, and at their best when they are singing.

I shall never forget the first time I saw a Botticelli angel, not in a vision, but on canvas. I had heard of him for years, of course, because in the time and place we have the misfortune to inhabit, the names of things are known to thousands who will never know (or before they have known), the thing itself. But the thing itself, the innocence of the Botticelli angel, struck me like a shaft of light when I came round the corner of a room in a house where I expected nothing but boredom, and suddenly saw that face. For you must note that, so far as pictures are concerned, innocence is expressed through the glance, and, indeed, I would rather remember innocent eyes than anything else. They are the loveliest of all lovely things—though I say it that shouldn't, for I have written in my time a line in which certain eyelids were called "the loveliest of all lovely things," and I still hope I was not wrong. Eyelids, you will remark, are the very negation of eyes. It is their business to come down like a shutter and deprive us of the eyes, whether innocent or green. But anyhow the line, though it was verse, was not true (something, alas! common to verse as a rule). It is eyes, I say, in which you will discover innocence more than in any other feature of the human beast.

And talking of beasts, beasts also have a sort of parody of innocence about them sometimes, but it

is never real innocence. No, not even in a certain
kitten which I know better than most kittens, and
which bears the name of Hitler. It is a grey kitten
with a heavenly blue in its gaze. Elephants have wise
eyes, though a little perky. And lions and most dogs
have plaintive eyes, and cattle have stupid eyes. No
beast has really innocent eyes, though some of them
come near to it.

* * *

Those who, in my trade of writing, have pulled off
the effect of innocence, have never been able to do
it save in flashes. It would seem to be like the sun,
which you cannot look full in the face—and Vau-
venargues said the same thing of death. You express
innocence by a side phrase, by a chance epithet, or
not at all. No description gives it, no drawing of
character, nor any fiddle-faddle of that sort—and
very rarely indeed does the word suggesting real innocence discover itself.

I have seen it in sculpture, and so, I suppose, has
every man. The divinest I know of is at Brou, where
it is very rightly evoked in the face of St. Mary
Magdalen. For it may be taken that hers is the type
of innocence recovered, and to recover innocence
requires a miracle. But Brou itself is a miracle, or
rather a collection of miracles. I was told once how
many statues there are in that amazing little desolate
chapel. I have forgotten the number—I know it is
many hundreds—and I take the Magdalen to be the
loveliest of the lot.

Then, I have seen innocence in the infant bas-relief of Goujon, and in more than one Donatello, notably in a glorious Donatello of the public gallery at Berlin; which gallery is almost the only thing worth seeing in that inadequate town, for no man would call the Avenue of Victory worth seeing, and there is certainly no innocence about *that*, save in the ironic sense, as attaching to the unfortunate sculptors who there exhibit their ineptitude. But then, protection was at work and no foreigners were allowed to compete.

Innocence has been expressed in music, and I for my part have felt it most in Mozart; but it is not for me to say anything about music, which has become of late a special study for experts, and of which (in that sense) I know nothing.

A smile will express innocence, but then a smile is not a work of art, or at least, when it is, it is a million miles from innocence. But of human handiwork I still return to the doctrine that innocence has been presented only by the painters, and by these, I think, very rarely.

So it would seem that innocence is a gem, a hidden treasure, rarely to be brought to light, and something too precious for mankind, or at any rate for the common possession of mankind. That is a pity, is it not?

THE END

76
77
79
83
85